DICKENS

A TALE OF
TWO CITIES

NOTES

COLES EDITORIAL BOARD

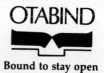

Bound to stay open

Publisher's Note

Otabind (Ota-bind). This book has been bound using the patented Otabind process. You can open this book at any page, gently run your finger down the spine, and the pages will lie flat.

ABOUT COLES NOTES

COLES NOTES have been an indispensible aid to students on five continents since 1948.

COLES NOTES are available for a wide range of individual literary works. Clear, concise explanations and insights are provided along with interesting interpretations and evaluations.

Proper use of COLES NOTES will allow the student to pay greater attention to lectures and spend less time taking notes. This will result in a broader understanding of the work being studied and will free the student for increased participation in discussions.

COLES NOTES are an invaluable aid for review and exam preparation as well as an invitation to explore different interpretive paths.

COLES NOTES are written by experts in their fields. It should be noted that any literary judgement expressed herein is just that – the judgement of one school of thought. Interpretations that diverge from, or totally disagree with any criticism may be equally valid.

COLES NOTES are designed to supplement the text and are not intended as a substitute for reading the text itself. Use of the NOTES will serve not only to clarify the work being studied, but should enhance the readers enjoyment of the topic.

ISBN 0-7740-3378-9

© COPYRIGHT 2000 AND PUBLISHED BY
COLES PUBLISHING COMPANY
TORONTO - CANADA
PRINTED IN CANADA

Manufactured by Webcom Limited
Cover finish: Webcom's Exclusive **DURACOAT**

CONTENTS

Charles Dickens: Life and Works

Charles John Huffam Dickens was born February 7, 1812, in Portsea (now Portsmouth), England. He was the second of eight children born to Elizabeth (Barrow) Dickens and John Dickens, a poorly paid navy pay office clerk. From the age of two to five years, Charles lived in London with his family, where his mother coached him in English and Latin. From the age of six to ten years, the family lived in Chatham, where Charles attended a school run by William Giles, the son of a Baptist minister. In 1823, the family moved to London where Charles spent much time exploring the streets which later became scenes for his novels.

As John Dickens found himself unable to meet his mounting debts (like the immortal Micawber of *David Copperfield*), Elizabeth Dickens attempted to supplement her husband's income by opening a private school for young children—but her efforts were unsuccessful. Charles went to work in a blacking warehouse when he was only 12 years old. Early in 1824, John Dickens was imprisoned for debt at Marshalsea (notoriously portrayed in *Little Dorrit*). Elizabeth Dickens and the six youngest children joined him in the debtors' prison while Charles stayed in a rooming house in London, supporting himself on his shilling-a-day earnings. Dickens described his work in this way:

> It was to cover the pots of paste blacking first with a piece of white paper and then with a piece of blue paper, to tie them round with a string, and then to clip the paper close and neat all round until it looked as smart as a pot of ointment from an apothecary's shop.

He did his work in front of the window and people used to stop and look at him. Dickens hated this and used to shudder with embarrassment. To make matters worse, as in *David Copperfield*, the other boys were rough.

> No words can express the secret agony of my soul, as I sank into this companionship. I worked from morning till night with common men and boys, a shabby child. I know that I tried but ineffectually not to anticipate my money and make it last through the week. I know I have lunged through the streets insufficiently clad and unsatisfactorily fed. I know but for the mercy of God, I might easily have been, for any care that was taken of me, a little robber or a little vagabond.

All this left a deep impression on Dickens' mind and this was reflected in his works. Most of the important child characters in his stories had similarly unpleasant childhoods.

While employed at the blacking factory, lodgings of a sort were provided for him. But for the rest, Dickens had to support himself on a very small wage of 6 shillings a week. With no money to go anywhere and little to do, Dickens spent his leisure hours wandering around London, an experience which was to serve him well in the writing of his novels later on. In them, he described not only the imposing places in London, but also the grimy back alleys such as the home of that frightening villain in *Oliver Twist*, Bill Sykes. Dickens acquired a knowledge of London and London life that was second to none, but the blacker side of London life is the more prominent in his novels; the slums in *Bleak House* rather than the fashionable promenades of the West End.

Luckily for Dickens, his father was released from the Marshalsea after six months, after inheriting a legacy enabling him to pay off his debts. Soon after his release, Mr. Dickens quarrelled with the owner of the blacking factory and Charles was dismissed. He went back to school happily, this time to the Wellington Academy at Hampstead. One of his schoolmates said that he was a handsome, curly-headed lad, full of life and fun, and probably was connected with every mischievous prank in the school. During this time he began to write tales which he passed around among the other boys and here, too, he developed a love of amateur theatricals which remained with him all his life, for he was a born actor.

Dickens' love of amateur theatricals led him to arrange private shows for his family and friends. He longed to be a professional actor. He might have fulfilled this ambition later on in his early twenties had not a bad cold prevented him from going to an interview with the stage manager of Covent Garden. At that time, anyway, he had begun to do rather well as a reporter and gave up the idea. But when he left school, at the age of 15, he found himself as a lawyer's clerk, tending to the petty cash ledger.

Dickens' immediate ambition on leaving school changed to that of becoming a reporter, as his father had done on leaving prison. With typical determination, he set out to fit himself for the post, teaching himself shorthand and studying in the evenings at the British Museum. As a result of this, Dickens obtained a job as a shorthand writer in the Courts of Doctors Commons (that is to say, the Law Courts, "Doctors" referring here to Doctors of Law). Here, once again, Dickens was to use his experiences later in his novels. In *A Tale of Two Cities* and *Great Expectations*, the Inns of Court are used, while in *Pickwick Papers* and again in *A Tale of Two Cities*, there are well-known trial scenes. He himself worked in Gray's Inn and it was there that he came to know the ways of lawyers and he speaks of the neighborhood of Chancery as if he knew every stone of its courts and alleys.

When Dickens was 22, he thought it would be more exciting to be a general reporter, and he obtained a job on *The Morning Chronicle* at a salary of 5 guineas a week. He was sent all over the country, from Edinburgh to Exeter. He thoroughly enjoyed every moment of it. As a boy, he'd often gone cold and hungry, but now he could arrive at night at a comfortable hotel, order a good meal, and relax in front of a good fire. But a reporter's life in those days was not all fun and games, for Dickens was a conscientious worker and his work came first.

> I have been in my time belated on miry byroads towards the small hours 40 or 50 miles from London in a wheelless carriage with exhausted horses and drunken postboys, and have got back in time for publication, to be received with never-to-be-forgotten compliments by my editor.

It was Dickens' custom to draw his characters from life and place them in situations and surroundings with which he was familiar. In the same way, many of the exciting scenes that are found in the novels spring from Dickens' experiences as a newspaperman. Anyone who's read the descriptions of scenes such as the shipwreck at Yarmouth in *David Copperfield* will realize what a fine reporter he was. This fact did not escape his editors and before long he was being kept in reserve to be sent on important emergency assignments at a moment's notice. His reports, like his novels, had vividness, gusto and a sense of humor, so different from the rather bloodless and factual reports in so many newspapers of the day.

In 1833, Dickens published in the *Monthly Magazine* his first work of fiction, *Dinner at Poplar Walk* (later reprinted as *Mr. Minns and His Cousin*). The following year, Dickens published additional sketches in this journal, as well as in the *Morning Chronicle* and its affiliate, the *Evening Chronicle*. In 1836, all of these short pieces were published together as *Sketches by Boz*. Dickens used the pen name of "Boz" (suggested by his brother's pronunciation of "Moses" while he had a cold). During 1836-37, under the sponsorship of the Chapman and Hall publishing firm, Dickens wrote the serial, *Pickwick Papers*, a humorous, episodic narrative which became widely popular.

Dickens always wrote from experience or deep knowledge of his city. He was a thorough and accurate observer. If he had but a scanty knowledge of his story, he would take great pains to obtain fuller details at first hand. For example, before writing *Nicholas Nickleby*, which was published in 1838, he made sure of his facts by travelling to Yorkshire, where he visited various boarding schools under the pretext of looking for a school for the son of a friend. One school he visited was the Bowes Academy, for he'd read that its headmaster had been in court for cruelty. Here he found the brutal atmosphere that is recaptured in the descriptions of Dotheboys Hall in *Nicholas Nickleby*.

In April of 1836, Dickens married Catherine Hogarth, whose father was a music critic and editor of the *Evening Chronicle*. In the late 1830's, Dickens established himself as a social reformer when, as editor of the monthly, *Bentley's Miscellany*, he published *The Mudfrog Papers* and *Oliver Twist* (1837-39). The latter work presented an incriminating picture of the workhouse and the foundling home, thereby attacking the Poor Law and the conduct of charitable institutions. During this period, Dickens was working at a characteristically feverish literary pace, producing such lesser works as *Sketches of Young Gentlemen* (1838) and *Sketches of Young Couples* (1840).

In 1840, Dickens edited the weekly, *Master Humphrey's Clock*, for which he wrote the serials *The Old Curiosity Shop* (1840-41) and *Barnaby Rudge* (1841). Since international copyright regulations were not yet established, Dickens' works were pirated in America. Partially, perhaps out of revenge, he wrote *American Notes* (1842) which contained unfavorable comments on American manners and institutions, and the practice of slavery. Further criticisms were directed at Americans in *Martin Chuzzlewit* (1843-44), a comic satire.

The first of Dickens' Christmas books, *A Christmas Carol*, appeared in 1843, followed by *The Chimes* (1844), *The Cricket on the Hearth* (1845), *The Battle of Life* (1846), and *The Haunted Man* (1848).

From 1844 to 1846, the Dickens family (now grown to five) lived alternately in Italy, Switzerland, and France. Out of this itinerant period came *Pictures from Italy* (1844-45) and *Dombey and Son* (1846-48), which attacked family pride and the worship of wealth. On his return to England in 1847, Dickens organized an amateur theatrical company in which he served as manager and principal actor. In 1851, the group was joined by Wilkie Collins, a prominent playwright and novelist who became Dickens' close friend and collaborator.

David Copperfield (1849-50) reflected a semi-autobiographical account of Dickens' own rise from obscurity to fame. Departing from his earlier farcical caricatures and exaggerations, it marked an artistic advance for the author. In 1850, Dickens and William Henry Wills started *Household Words*, a weekly journal taking a reformist political position. In it appeared *A Child's History of England* (1851-53), *Bleak House* (1852-53), which attacks the chancery courts and the slums around Chancery Lane, and *Little Dorrit* (1855-57), which is a satire of Victorian England.

Dickens' love of acting was one of the great passions of his life. At Christmas in 1853, Dickens gave his first public readings in Birmingham Town Hall, in aid of the establishment of a Birmingham and Midland Institute which would give greater educational opportunities for the working people. There was a natural choice of what to read in *A Christmas Carol*. Dickens wrote to the organizers:

There would be some novelty in the thing as I've never done it in public, though I have in private and, if I may say so, with a great effect on the hearers.

And it was with great effect that he read that night. It was so successful that he was asked to give a second reading three days later. This he consented to do on condition that it should be a working people's night, with cheap seats that working people could afford.

I never saw, nor do I suppose anyone ever did, such a moving sight as the working people's night. There were 2,500 of them there and a more delicately observant audience it is impossible to imagine. They lost nothing, misinterpreted nothing, followed everything closely, laughed and cried with the most delightful correctness.

Dickens frequently visited Birmingham. Once he was there with some friends after a visit to Shakespeare's birthplace at Stratford, and Dr. Johnson's at Lichfield. They stopped longer than expected and ran short of ready cash. They were forced to pawn their gold watches with a Birmingham jeweller. His friends thought this hardly dignified but Dickens could afford to laugh at it. He probably remembered the times as a boy when he had been sent to the pawnshop after dark so that the neighbors would not see, but now with wealth and fame behind him, it was just a huge joke, for who cared who knew?

When he was a boy in Chatham, Dickens had dreamed of buying Gad's Hill Place near Rochester. Once again he was able to fulfill a childhood amibition, for, in 1856, he bought it and lived there most of the time from 1860 until his death.

It gave him a thrill that the house was situated on Shakespeare's Gad's Hill, mentioned in *Henry IV,* Part I. Dickens put up a plaque on the first floor landing:

This house, Gad's Hill Place, stands on the site of Shakespeare's Gad's Hill, ever memorable for its association with Sir John Falstaff in his noble fancy.

Gad's Hill Place was generally full of company, fun and laughter. Later on, Dickens bought the meadow behind the house which he allowed to be used for cricket and other games. A nearby cricket club was allowed to make it their own ground. He also sponsored athletic sports on the meadow for which he provided the prizes. Once again he was successful in his ventures, for one year 2,000 people turned up. Actually, Dickens was not much of a sportsman himself but he was never too busy to help in a good cause.

The joy of Gad's Hill Place was marred for Dickens and his wife by growing marital unhappiness. By 1858, a legal separation was agreed upon and his sister-in-law, Georgina Hogarth, managed Dickens' household affairs from then until his death. Concurrent with the separation, and due to a rift with the part owners of *Household Words*, Dickens and Wills dissolved the periodical and launched in its place, *All the Year Round*. To insure the magazine's success, the first issue began the weekly serial of *A Tale of Two Cities*, followed by other serials including *The Uncommercial Traveller* (1860) which was a commentary on foreign and domestic issues, and *Great Expectations* (1860-61), another semi-autobiographical novel.

Dickens gave public readings from 1859 to 1868 in London, Scotland, and America, which added substantially to his income. His last completed novel was *Our Mutual Friend* (1864-65), another social satire. This was followed by two shorter works published in America by James Thomas Fields: *A Holiday Romance* (1868) which was a children's story, and *George Silverman's Explanation* (1868) which sneered at dissenters.

Back at Gad's Hill Place in 1870, Dickens began work on a suspense tale, *The Mystery of Edwin Drood*. Shortly after completing his sixth instalment, he collapsed in the dining room of his home. He died the following morning, June 9, at the age of 58, and was buried at Westminster Abbey. His request for a simple grave near his last home was ignored.

The characters he created have become personal friends to his many readers through the years. Dickens gave to us a warm, rich and full world, a world such as it is, full of the good and the bad, but always full of hope for the future. He was a man of the ordinary folk. It was about ordinary folk that he wrote and to them he gave the rich world of his imagination.

Introduction to *A Tale of Two Cities*

In his preface to the novel, Dickens states:

Whenever any reference (however slight) is made here to the condition of the French people before or during the Revolution, it is truly made, on the faith of trustworthy witnesses. It has been one of my hopes to add something to the popular and picturesque means of understanding that terrible time, though no one can hope to add anything to the philosophy of Mr. Carlyle's wonderful book.

What Dickens believed was that in writing about the past, it is not the function of a novelist to simply portray history, but to recreate it.

In considering the genesis of *A Tale of Two Cities*, we must look to the "Mr. Carlyle" mentioned in the "Preface." This was the great Scottish social essayist and historian, Thomas Carlyle. Carlyle's book, *The French Revolution*, was published in 1837, and Dickens read it avidly, extracting from it the bulk of his background information for the novel. It is said that he asked Carlyle for some of the reference material alluded to in *The French Revolution* and that the Scotsman, with good humor, forwarded "about two cart-loads." Dickens took the matter seriously, and it is reported that he read it all. The style of *The French Revolution* was strongly pictorial, and this was certainly compatible with Dickens' own vivid quality of writing. He was greatly moved by Carlyle's social philosophy, and *A Tale of Two Cities* can be recognized as an outgrowth of Carlyle's work, a type of dramatic extension of it.

Historical Background

In the opening chapter of Book I of *A Tale of Two Cities,* Dickens allots about equal space to the problems of England and of France in 1775, and he implies that the two cities of London and Paris will be equally treated in the narrative. In Book II, Dickens satirizes English justice, lawyers, and courts of law, and divides the time almost evenly between France and England, but clearly it is the problems of France that fascinate him. In Book III, Dickens focusses almost entirely on the Reign of Terror in France. This is one of history's most significant periods, for from it dates our modern era. Serious scholars, philosophers, historians, novelists, poets, readers in search of excitement—all have found this period fascinating and have felt impelled to go backward in history to the times that produced the upheaval. The student reading *A Tale of Two Cities* would do well to reinforce his study of the novel with a review of eighteenth-century France and note with what discrimination Dickens selected details to achieve his purpose.

France entered the eighteenth century a disturbed and shaken nation. In the seventeenth century, Louis XIV had set in motion the social forces that were to ruin France at the same time that, as a patron of the arts, he created the atmosphere in which flourished the artists and artisans who were to produce enduring monuments in architecture, sculpture, painting, and literature. When Louis XIV decided to transfer the court from Paris to Versailles, so that he might indulge his love of hunting, he had the château at Versailles expanded to include a vast and magnificent complex of structures where five thousand courtiers lived in an opulence that ruined the nation. Worse still, it ruined the nobles. In earlier times, the nobles had been responsible for furnishing troops to defend the kingdom and, in return for their service, they were exempted from taxation. Under Louis XIV the nobles no longer had this responsibility, they no longer exercised power, but they did preserve their privilege of exemption from taxation. Taxes fell on the poor.

In Paris, the bourgeoisie prospered and, in the conduct of its social life, mimicked court life at Versailles. As at Versailles, the great names in literature and art flourished, and life was lived splendidly. In the provinces, want and prosperity existed side by side. It was probably the most brilliant period in all of French literature, led by Molière, acknowledged to be the greatest name in French literature. The two leading tragic dramatists were Corneille and Racine. Students of French will know that on the roster also belong Bossuet, Pascal, La Fontaine, and Fenelon. Among the famed artists and decorators, the architects and sculptors are most noteworthy, among whom are Hardouin-Mansart, the architect of Versailles and LeNôtre, who planned the gardens of Versailles. The king's manner of living and ruling created greatness, but it was the kind of greatness that weakened the financial and political structure and made possible, if not inevitable, a revolution. It is said that the people, made bankrupt and disconsolate by the king's policies, rejoiced when he died in 1715. He had once said, *"Après moi, le deluge."* The deluge came within seventy-five years.

Under Louis XV the country continued its ruinous course, characterized by intrigue and corruption within the court, extravagance of life at court, loss of the French colonies in the New World, destruction of the French navy, further weakening of the powers of the nobility and the clergy, bigotry, rising debts, and heavier taxation. All of these factors combined to reduce France to the status of a second-class power politically, although her prestige remained high.

Other influences were also at work. Alone among the countries of Europe, France permitted freedom of expression. Only in France could have spread the ideas which would inflame the people to organize and to revolt. A brilliant group of intellectuals attacked bigotry and prejudice, injustice, the clergy, and the monarchy. Of this group the two greatest were Voltaire and Rousseau. Voltaire, brilliant novelist, historian, scientist, biographer, and philosopher, was the colorful master spirit of the age, attacking privilege, oppression, and injustice and pleading for education, tolerance, and liberty. In 1762, Jean-Jacques Rousseau, another genius of great range and scope, proclaimed in his *Contrat Social* the sovereignty of the people and argued for freedom and equality. His most famous line, "Man is born free, but everywhere he is in irons," may express a basic fallacy, but it has a ring that caught the public's fancy. Rousseau's teachings inflamed men and women with the spirit of revolution.

A succession of finance ministers could find no way of solving the worsening financial structure of France. With the nobility and clergy still exempt from taxation, all new methods of extorting money were applied to the people. A system of letting out contracts for collection of taxes to greedy financiers, called farmers-general, brought in money but further fanned public discontent. In the midst of threatening disaster and bankruptcy, the nobles and the court pursued their pleasures. In all of Europe the French language was the language of the aristocracy. (Compare with Dickens' chapters "Monseigneur in Town," "Monseigneur in the Country," and "The Gorgon's Head.")

In 1774, Louis XVI inherited the throne and all the woes of the nation. A timid, honest ruler, he sincerely wanted to do away with abuses, but he had no real interest in politics. He had two interests, hunting and playing at his hobby of locksmithing. (Compare with Dr. Manette's finding solace in making shoes.) At the age of sixteen he married Marie Antoinette, his much-maligned, misunderstood queen with a need for love, a passion for gaiety, and a gift for making enemies. Influenced by her mother, the Empress of Austria, to advance the interests of Austria at the French court, she made herself suspect, and her enemies used every opportunity she gave them to discredit her and turn her good qualities to her disadvantage. The king appointed an able finance minister, but trouble arose when he proposed reforms. Had the needed reforms been accomplished, that is, the taxing of the privileged classes, the Revolution might have been averted. Lafayette wrote in 1787 that there was "a strange contrast between the king's despotic powers, the courtiers' conniving and servility and the extraordinary freedom of language and criticism." Louis XVI was an absolute but liberal monarch.

In 1788, the country as a whole seemed not to be wretched but comfortably well off. What the people wanted was for the king to preside at necessary reforms, to hold in check the privileged classes, and to tax their wealth. They were satisfied with a monarchy but they wanted the old medieval economy replaced. They wanted power transferred from the class that was no longer capable of exercising power to the now cultured and educated middle class, the Third Estate. The king had granted people the freedom to complain. Had he supported the Third Estate against the privileged classes he could have saved France from revolution and could have saved the monarchy. France saw what had been accomplished in America. But what Lafayette, who had observed the American Revolution, and other Frenchmen could not see was the difference between the American colonists and the French. The American colonists, through the American town meeting, had prepared for a government of and by the people, and they had conservative leaders, such as George Washington, who had been able to keep the American Revolution under control. In fact, in the long history of revolutions, the American Revolution is unique. The French people, having no understanding of a constitutional government, wanted a republic without knowing what a republic was. So, the French Revolution, once launched, became a series of frenzied riots with intervals of calm. (Compare with Dickens' "Echoing Footsteps," "The Sea Still Rises," and "Fire Rises.")

In 1789, under edict of the king, the States General met at Versailles in May and there was hope. Over 900 deputies convened, altogether an assemblage of men of high moral and intellectual qualities. In June, the 500 deputies chosen to represent the Third Estate, joined by members of the lower clergy and many of the nobles, proclaimed themselves the National Assembly and voted that taxation without consent was illegal. This act, usurping the power of the king, began the Revolution. The king had to decide whether to support the people or the privileged classes. He took the part of the nobles and asked his foreign troops to come to Paris and Versailles to defend him. Rumors spread through Paris that quantities of powder had been transferred to the Bastille, and on the next day, July 14, the crowd stormed the Bastille, the symbol of feudalism, killed the governor and the guards, and rioted in the streets. (Compare Dickens' "Echoing Footsteps.") This demonstration was the first of the revolutionary demonstrations, each of which left its imprint on the nation. This defiance of the king struck a decisive blow to his prestige. In the provinces, fear drove the people to chaos and anarchy. Châteaux, tax offices and jails were set on fire in local uprisings. In August, many nobles and members of the clergy emigrated. Many others relinquished their feudal privileges and the people were heartened. The assembly proclaimed human rights in a *Declaration of the Rights of Man and of the Citizen* and retained the king. (Compare Dickens' "Fire Rises.")

In October, 1789, several thousand women marched on Versailles, demanding that the assembly meet in Paris and that the king live in Paris. In February, 1790, the king accepted the principles of the Revolution, but there was no governing body. Then the assembly set about to create a constitution. In July, 1790, on the anniversary of the fall of the Bastille, there was promise of order, but less than a year later the royal family tried to flee. They were captured at Varennes and were returned to the palace of the Tuileries in Paris to live as prisoners, the king by his action having forfeited all semblance of prestige. In September, the assembly completed the constitution, which the king accepted, declaring, "The goal of the Revolution has been reached." Its work completed, the assembly disbanded, but new revolutions were to come.

The new assembly, called the Legislative, was chosen, composed of conflicting factions and lacking experienced leadership. One group, more famous for its orators than for action, the Girondists, joined the king in favoring a war against Austria. The king hoped to save the monarchy by winning a victory over the Austrians. In April, 1792, war was declared against Austria, and Prussia joined Austria. In July, the enemy issued a manifesto, threatening France with destruction if the royal family were not shown respect. The Parisian mob decided that it was time to be rid of the king and, in August, they attacked the Tuileries. A revolutionary tribunal was set up. (Compare Dickens' "Triumph.") There followed the infamous September massacres during which over 1,200 prisoners perished at the hands of the murdering rioters. (Compare Dickens' "The Grindstone.") Meanwhile, the invading armies were turned back. The Legislative Assembly disbanded and another group took over, the National Convention. In January, 1793, the king was tried and beheaded. In October, Marie Antoinette followed him to the guillotine.

One by one the revolutionary leaders succeeded each other and met death. Danton and Madame Roland were guillotined, and Marat was stabbed in his bathtub. One tyranny yielded to another. By 1793, the Reign of Terror was in full swing. (Compare Dickens' "The Wood-Sawyer," "The Game Made," "Darkness," "Fifty-two," "The Knitting Done," "The Footsteps Die Out Forever.") For fourteen months it went on without recess until July, 1794, when the last of the revolutionary tyrants, Robespierre, was overthrown, and the indiscriminate butcheries came to an end. Thousands had perished—men of letters, scientists, the great and the small, old men and women in their eighties, young girls in their teens, most of them victims of baseless accusations, many merely suspects, and finally the guillotiners themselves were guillotined. Paris had by this time lost its taste for guillotining as a festive occasion.

In the midst of these terrors, life in Paris went on calmly, though cautiously, for most of its 650,000 inhabitants, many of whom were well-to-do. Like the Manettes, they made no display of material wealth, but there were many theaters to attend. About 30,000 could be classed as poor.

The age that created the Revolution (and the Revolution itself) has always exerted a powerful fascination upon the imagination of historians and writers. Students still read the dramas, novels, and poetry of these times. France has preserved the sites and symbols of the monarchy and the Revolution. Visitors marvel at the splendor of Versailles, the colonnade of the Louvre, the glories of its art treasures, the beauty of the Place de la Concorde, where the guillotine once stood. They shudder at the gruesome reminders of the prisoners in the Conciergerie, at the sight of the bell that announced the arrival of the tumbrils, now in the Women's Courtyard in the Conciergerie. They visit homes, prisons, rooms, streets, monuments, the Place de la Bastille, the faubourg Saint Antoine—all identified with people or events of the Revolution, friends and foes sharing equally in making their country's history. The men and women of these periods were educated and articulate. They have left behind not only their formal and published writings, but a great volume of letters, memoirs, and diaries. The prisons kept detailed information on each prisoner, so that a remarkable body of information exists about the thousands who died at the guillotine.

What happened to the émigrés who started to leave France in 1789 is the subject of many books. (Compare Dickens' "Drawn to the Loadstone Rock.") Many had the foresight to transfer their wealth and valuables out of France, but more were fortunate to escape with their lives. Altogether, about 120,000 émigrés fled, about half of them members of the Third Estate, whose property excited the mob's greed. The rest were members of the aristocracy and their devoted servants, and members of the clergy. About 25,000 sought refuge in London. Many were welcomed by relatives and friends, expecting that their exile would last for a few months at the most. But many were destitute. To assist them, emergency committees were established in England and continued to function for over twenty years.

A Tale of Two Cities is the second of Charles Dickens' historical novels (the less popular one was *Barnaby Rudge*, published in 1841). It was begun when the author was forty-seven years old, and shortly after his separation from his wife. Dickens had been editor of *Household Words* until 1858. This journal was one-quarter owned by the publishers Bradbury and Evans, also the proprietors of *Punch*. When *Punch* would not carry a brief explanation of Dickens' rift with his wife, he retaliated by dissolving *Household Words* and launching its successor, *All the Year Round*. To insure the magazine's success, *A Tale of Two Cities* was begun with the first issue, April 30, 1859, and was continued in weekly instalments until November 26.

The novel attempts to delineate the social evils in France culminating in the conflict between the aristocracy and the laboring classes. The nobility is cynical, arrogant, and cruel. The rising peasantry is uncouth and violent. But this is a picture of action by and between individuals, and no attempt is made to explain the intellectual causes of the French Revolution—the *class war for power* between the reactionary feudal lords and the rising bourgeoisie as France's economy was transformed from an agricultural one to an industrialized one. The conclusion one might draw from Dickens' presentation is that the French Revolution, like all violent revolutions, was neither good nor bad—it was *necessary* to the forward thrust of history. The lack of a sweeping philosophy is what, perhaps, accounts for the wide and continuing popularity of *A Tale of Two Cities*. Very few people are aware of the transcendental aspects of the historical period in which they live. The majority, like the characters in Dickens' novel, are aware only of the effects of social upheavals upon their own status and daily lives.

Plot Summary

Book I opens in 1775. Corruption reigns in both England and France.

Mr. Jarvis Lorry and Lucie Manette travel from England to France in order to gain custody of Lucie's father, Dr. Alexandre Manette, who has been a prisoner in the Bastille for the past eighteen years and is now being sheltered by his former servant, Monsieur Defarge. When they find Dr. Manette, he is only a shadow of his former self. They return him to England to restore him to life.

Book II opens in London five years later. Lucie's love has revived her father's mental and physical health. Charles Darnay is being tried for treason. He is acquitted, largely because Sydney Carton points out the remarkable resemblance between himself and Darnay, thus discrediting the testimony that Charles was seen passing information to the enemy.

Sydney Carton confesses his love to Lucie and vows to make any sacrifice for her and "for any dear" to her.

Charles Darnay's ruthless aristocratic uncle, the Marquis D'Evrémonde, kills under the wheels of his carriage the child of Gaspard, a peasant in Saint Antoine. The next morning the Marquis is found murdered in his bed. One year passes after the death of Gaspard's child and the murder of the Marquis. Gaspard, who had murdered the Marquis, has been found and executed. Madame Defarge "registers" into her knitting the name of Evrémonde and all his race as doomed to destruction. When she learns that Charles Darnay is the nephew of the late Marquis, she "registers" the name of Charles Darnay.

On July 14, 1789, the peasants storm the Bastille. Charles Darnay decides to return to France to help an old family servant in distress.

In France, Darnay is imprisoned as an "emigrant." One year later, he is acquitted, but that same day he is imprisoned again, denounced by the Defarges and "one other." At this trial, a document written by Dr. Manette in 1767 when he was a prisoner in the Bastille is read. It reveals that Charles' father and his father's brother (the Marquis D'Evrémonde) were responsible for the deaths of Madame Defarge's entire family and for Dr. Manette's imprisonment. Charles is sentenced to die.

Sydney Carton gains admittance into Charles' cell, drugs him, and goes to the guillotine in his place. His last words are: "It is a far, far better thing that I do, than I have ever done; it is a far, far better rest that I go to, than I have ever known."

Characters in the Novel

DR. ALEXANDRE MANETTE: Imprisoned for eighteen years because of his sympathies toward the oppressed French peasantry, he loses his sanity and takes to compulsive shoemaking. Reunited with his daughter, he is restored through her devotion to health, happiness, and usefulness.

LUCIE MANETTE: Dr. Manette's daughter. Her deep sincerity, devotion to duty, and subtle personal charm arouse the deep, abiding love of Charles Darnay (whom she marries) and the worshipping, self-sacrificing love of Sydney Carton (who dies for her).

CHARLES DARNAY: Husband of Lucie. He is twice saved from death through his remarkable resemblance to Sydney Carton.

SYDNEY CARTON: An alcoholic and self-indulgent man whose love for Lucie climaxes in his giving his life to save that of her husband.

JARVIS LORRY: Connected with Tellson's Bank which has offices in London and Paris. He is a lifelong friend of the Manettes and, at the conclusion of the story, aids in the escape from France of Lucie and Charles.

JERRY CRUNCHER: Also connected with Tellson's Bank. Though of lower social status than Jarvis Lorry, he is equally loyal and faithful to the Manettes—though a brutal and unkind husband to his wife.

MARQUIS D'EVRÉMONDE: Uncle of Charles Darnay and stereotype of the rich, arrogant, and selfish French nobleman.

ERNEST DEFARGE: A wineshop owner in St. Antoine. In his youth he was a servant to Dr. Manette and retains his loyalty to the family through the years, boarding the old man when he is first released from prison.

THERESE DEFARGE: Wife of the wineshop owner. A crude and vengeful woman, she dominates her husband and tries to prevent the escape of the Darnays from France.

STRYVER: A friend and associate of Sydney Carton; also Darnay's defence counsel in the English treason trial.

MISS PROSS: Lucie's governess and, later, housekeeper for the Darnay-Manette household.

JOHN BARSAD: A spy and informer, Barsad's real identity is Solomon Pross, brother of Miss Pross.

ROGER CLY: Darnay's former servant who is an associate and co-spy of John Barsad.

AGGERAWAYTER: Overly pious wife of Jerry Cruncher.

YOUNG JERRY: Son of Jerry and Aggerawayter Cruncher.

LITTLE LUCIE: Daughter of Lucie and Charles Darnay.

THEOPHILE GABELLE: Family servant and tax collector for the Marquis D'Evrémonde. Gabelle's imprisonment is the cause of Darnay's fateful return to France.

SOLOMON: Brother of Miss Pross (see John Barsad).

MONSEIGNEUR: A name Dickens uses for any French overlord whose exact identity is unimportant to the plot.

JACQUES ONE, TWO AND THREE: Friends of Defarge; co-conspirators in plotting the Revolution.

The Time Element

Much attention is given to details of dates to connect the story with historical events and to give the impression of reality to the fictional part.

The entire narrative covers thirty-five years, from Dr. Manette's arrest to the execution of Louis XVI, 1757-1793, while the actual story occupies eighteen years, 1775-1793. The date of Carton's death is not clearly stated, but since that of Louis and Marie Antoinette is reported before it, it must have been in 1793, the year of mass executions in Paris.

1757, December 22: Dr. Manette summoned by the Evrémonde brothers to a patient.

1757, December 31: Imprisonment of Manette in the Bastille.

1758: Birth of Lucie.

1767: Miss Pross enters Lucie's service.

1767, December 31: Manette completes his written statement in the Bastille.

1775, November: Release of Manette and opening of the story.

1781, Summer: Darnay's trial in London.

1780, Autumn: Miss Pross worried by the "hundreds" of visitors.

1781, Autumn: Murder of the Marquis D'Evrémonde.

1782, Autumn: Cruncher's disappointment over the body-snatching of Cly.

The mender of roads' account of the hanging of Gaspard.

1783: Marriage of Lucie and Darnay.

1783-1789: Six years of married life; birth of little Lucie and her brother.

1789, July 14: Capture of the Bastille.

1789, Autumn: Burning of the Evrémonde château.

1792: Darnay returns to Paris; is imprisoned in La Force.

1793, October: Lucie's signals to her husband.

1793, December: Darnay's first trial in Paris, acquittal, and re-arrest.

1793, January: Execution of Louis XVI, and of Marie Antoinette in October.

Darnay's sentence to the guillotine and substitution by Carton.

Chapter by Chapter
Summaries and Commentaries

Book I — Recalled to Life

CHAPTER 1

The Period

Summary

The year is 1775 and conditions in England and France are bad, but not any different from other periods in history. England is favored with spiritual revelations, but none so potent as the earthly revelations she receives from America.

France, under King Louis XVI and Queen Marie Antoinette, is bankrupt economically and religiously. Above all, her people treat each other inhumanely. Fate and Death foreshadow the awful Revolution that lies ahead.

Conditions are no better in England. Under King George III and Queen Charlotte Sophia, thievery and murder run rampant and the law has become a mockery of justice.

Commentary

The famous poetic lines that open the novel offer a dispassionate overview of the whole era of the French Revolution. With a mature and mellow perspective, Dickens sees all things at once, and accepts them as inevitable in the course of human events. In this way he sets the tone for the novel, a tone that will attempt to be objective, historical, and narrative.

At the time Dickens began to work on *A Tale of Two Cities*, he was afraid he was losing his public appeal. He had separated from his wife, and, because of a disagreement with his backers, had dissolved his magazine, *Household Words*. Therefore, when he immediately began a new magazine, *All the Year Round,* he wanted to serialize in it a novel that would "give [him his] old standing with [his] old public." He thought, rightly so, that a tightly woven plot with the emphasis on "incident" rather than "dialogue" would make the *Tale* "popular."

Chapter 1 contains a number of indirect and rather obscure references, making a complete understanding of it somewhat difficult to achieve.

The "king with a large jaw and a queen with a plain face, on the throne of England" are George III (1760-1820) and Charlotte Sophia (1761-1818). The "king with a large jaw and a queen with a fair face, on the throne of France" are Louis XVI and Marie Antoinette (1774-1793).

Dickens satirizes the English belief in the supernatural. "Mrs. Southcott" was Joanna Southcott (1750-1814) who, about 1792, began to claim the gift of prophecy. She said that, as the woman in Revelation 12, she would be the mother of the coming Messiah. Soon after the date she had set for the birth of the "second Shiloh," she died. Many people studied her tracts and books, and some people still do. The references to the "Cock-lane ghost" and "the spirits of this very year last past" further satirize belief in spirits. With tongue-in-cheek, Dickens speaks of "mere messages in the early order of events [that] had lately come to the English Crown and People," referring to the American Revolution.

Dickens continues in this sarcastic vein, now directing his satire towards France. He refers to the economic inflation and the political and religious corruption rampant in eighteenth-century France. But "it is likely enough," he says, that Fate and Death, with their guillotine and tumbrils, already lurk in the background, thus strongly foreshadowing the Revolution.

England is no better in 1775. Robbery and murder are everyday occurrences, and the law is a mere mockery of justice. Dickens' zeal for social reform and his hatred of injustice, so evident in all his works, show clearly here.

QUESTION: What mood does Dickens establish? How much historical and narrative background can you glean from these opening pages?

CHAPTER 2

The Mail

Summary

On a cold, fog-ridden night in November, 1775, the Dover mail coach laboriously makes its way toward Dover. As the three passengers are re-entering the coach, after walking up a hill to lighten the load for the weary horses struggling in the mud, a rider gallops up from the direction in which they had come, demanding to see one of the passengers, Mr. Jarvis Lorry, of Tellson's Bank, London. Distrustful, the coach guard covers the rider, but finally allows him to deliver a written message to Mr. Lorry, who has recognized him as "Jerry." By the light of the coach lamp Lorry reads: "Wait at Dover for Mam'selle." Lorry's puzzling reply is: "Jerry, say that my answer was, Recalled to Life." The coach resumes its lumbering journey, and the lone rider ponders the message as he returns to London.

Commentary

The "steaming mist" that roams "like an evil spirit" introduced a kind of imagery that Dickens uses throughout the novel, imagery that deals with death. Also, the "unwholesome sea" becomes a dominant image, especially when the hordes of French peasants overrun France like a huge tidal wave.

The mistrust and suspicion that everyone feels for everyone else (animals included)—such as those aboard the coach show toward Lorry and Jerry in this chapter—is indicative of the general antagonism that characterizes so many of the relationships in the novel.

Dickens' skilled craftsmanship is seen in Jerry Cruncher's first appearance. Very logically, he is covered with mud after his long, hard ride. As the novel progresses, mud and Jerry become more and more closely associated with each other until we learn what his occupation really is. We may note, too, that he appears out of the mist, the same mist that was "like an evil spirit." Thus, there is something death-like (or ghostly) associated with Jerry.

Mr. Lorry's puzzling answer, "Recalled to Life," is a significant phrase. Dickens seriously considered it as a title for this novel. An important theme concerning rebirth and resurrection is introduced here. Equally puzzling is Jerry's soliloquy after the coach passes on: "You'd be in a Blazing bad way, if recalling to life was to come into fashion, Jerry." Both puzzles are explained later in the novel.

QUESTION: Have you learned anything about Mr. Jarvis Lorry? What kind of a character is Jerry Cruncher?

CHAPTER 3

The Night Shadows

Summary

Just as every human creature keeps within him his own individual secrets, so do the messenger on horseback, Jerry Cruncher, and the passenger in the Dover mail coach, Mr. Jarvis Lorry. Riding back to Tellson's Bank where he will deliver the message "Recalled to Life," Jerry experiences more and more uneasiness as he rides into the shadows of the night.

Mr. Lorry, riding in the coach with the other two passengers, stares out into the darkness, envisioning a worn and wasted, prematurely white-haired, middle-aged man who always gives the same imaginary response to Mr. Lorry's persistent question, "Buried how long?": "Almost eighteen years." Lorry asks, "You know that you are recalled to life?" and then, "Shall I show her to you? Will you come and see her?" to which the vision gives negatives replies.

Dawn breaks, and as Lorry looks at the sun he says, "Gracious Creator of day! To be buried alive for eighteen years!"

Commentary

Some of Dickens' own unhappiness seems to reflect in the opening paragraph of this chapter. Although he was by now, at the age of forty-seven, a highly successful and respected writer, editor, and theatrical producer, his marriage was unsuccessful and he experienced deep frustration and loneliness. Also, perhaps because he had driven himself relentlessly for many years, writing countless novels and short pieces, acting and lecturing, his health was breaking down, causing him severe physical discomfort. He says that we never know the innermost secrets of the individual soul. In other words, although one may appear happy and successful on the surface, he may be an entirely different person underneath. He continues, too, his preoccupation with death, saying that life, like death, is inscrutable.

The theme "Recalled to Life" clearly enunciates itself as Mr. Lorry visualizes bringing to life again a death-like vision, cadaverous and prematurely white-haired, who has been "buried alive" for eighteen years. The symbolism of the rising sun, the coming day, and Mr. Lorry's explicit statement "Gracious Creator of day!" all point to a rebirth. However, the reader continues to be mystified regarding exactly what is happening in the story.

We do not learn until later that Jerry's last name is Cruncher, but we do learn something about his physical appearance. His eyes are set close together and have a sinister expression. His black, stiff hair grows jaggedly around his bald crown, and his nose is broad and blunt.

QUESTION: What is Mr. Lorry's association with Tellson's Bank? And what is the purpose of his journey in such forbidding weather?

CHAPTER 4

The Preparation

Summary

Mr. Lorry arrives at Dover. First he inquires whether there will be a packet ship to Calais the following day, and then he makes himself comfortable at the Royal George Hotel. Mr. Jarvis Lorry, a confidential, bachelor clerk at Tellson's Bank in London, is a fine figure of a sixty-year old gentleman. The brown clothes he wears to breakfast after his arrival are worn but well kept. Beneath a small flaxen wig that he wears, his expression, although seemingly cool and reserved, is lighted up "by a pair of moist bright eyes."

Towards night, the "Mam'selle" his message told him to expect arrives. She is Miss Lucie Manette, a pretty, blonde, blue-eyed young lady of "not more than seventeen," who has come from London. She informs Mr. Lorry that she received a letter from Tellson's Bank saying she must go to Paris and communicate with a gentleman from the bank regarding property of her dead father. Mr. Lorry says he is the gentleman despatched by the bank. Miss Manette says she was fearful of travelling to France alone, and the bank sent the messenger after Mr. Lorry so he would wait for her in Dover and accompany her to Paris. Mr. Lorry graciously agrees to do so.

Quite nervously and with many protests that this is all just "a matter of business," he tells Miss Manette the real reason why Tellson's Bank is sending her to France. Contrary to Miss Manette's belief that she has been an orphan since she was two, Mr. Lorry informs her that her father is living in Paris, that somehow he has been released from prison (the Bastille) where he has probably been confined for eighteen years, and that probably he is terribly changed and totally wrecked. When he disappeared, apparently imprisoned, his wife tried vainly to locate him. She thought it best for her daughter, Lucie, to think him dead. Tellson's Bank has been responsible for Dr. Manette's estate all these years, and it was Mr. Lorry himself who brought Lucie Manette to England after her mother's death when Lucie was but a child. Lorry is now being sent to Paris to identify her father, and she is being sent "to restore him to life, love, duty, rest, comfort." Their mission is highly secretive. They are to remove Dr. Manette out of France and bring him to London immediately.

The news proves too much of a shock for Miss Manette, and she falls into a trance. A "wild-looking woman," all in red, answers Mr. Lorry's loud call for assistance and, upon entering the room, simultaneously bawls out Mr. Lorry for frightening the young girl to death and administers tenderly to Miss Manette. Mr. Lorry asks her if she can accompany Miss Manette to France.

Commentary

Like the bank that he represents, Mr. Lorry is the very essence of respectability, stability and tradition. These traits will contrast significantly with the revolutionary traits of chaos and anarchy soon to erupt.

Lucie Manette is introduced in a setting suffused with death imagery, such as the tall candles seemingly buried in the mahogany. Even more significant, perhaps, is the sharp image of the pier-glass frame behind her. In the disfigurement and the offerings of the Negro cupids, Dickens seems to be making the point that love cannot be easily fulfilled. Sacrifice is necessary. In this case, the "headlessness" of the cupids is especially relevant, as we shall learn much later on. At the time that he wrote this novel, Dickens, separated from his wife, was infatuated with a young, blonde, blue-eyed actress named Ellen Ternan. He must have been profoundly disturbed by the complications of such a relationship and could see no easy or perfect fulfillment for it.

Despite the fussy "old bachelor" manner in which Mr. Lorry

conveys his story, he manages to underline it with warmth and sympathy. And the brawny, red-haired woman (who proves to be Miss Pross), who might strike the reader as a frightening demon at first, proves to be an invaluable friend.

QUESTION: Do you understand now the full significance of Mr. Lorry's message, "Recalled to Life"? What will the Manettes' new life be like?

CHAPTER 5

The Wine-Shop

Summary

A large wine cask has broken in a street of Saint Antoine, a district of Paris, and the starving peasants enjoy a few moments of frolicsome refreshment. With foreshadowing, the street and people are left stained red, and one of the peasants scrawled "BLOOD" on a wall with a wine-soaked finger.

Hunger stalks everywhere, attacking everyone, turning young people old and predetermining the fact that the time will come when blood instead of wine will be spilled in the streets of France. Foreshadowed, too, are the men who will be hauled up by ropes and pulleys "to flare upon the darkness of their condition," replacing the feebly lit *lanternes* that hang there today.

The master of the wine-shop, Monsieur Defarge, shrugs off the incident of the broken cask, but meaningfully admonishes the prankster, Gaspard, who had scrawled "BLOOD" on the wall, saying "is there no other place to write such words in?"—and he placed a hand on the man's heart. Monsieur Defarge is a solidly built, strong-looking man of thirty whose path or opinion you would not want to cross, "for nothing would turn the man."

Madame Defarge, his stout wife, also presents a solid front as she sits in the wine-shop with knitting in her lap and "a watchful eye." With a barely perceptible signal, she warns her returning husband that some new customers have come into the shop. His eyes find an elderly man and a young lady: Mr. Jarvis Lorry and Miss Lucie Manette.

Monsieur Defarge exchanges a few words with three of his customers, all four of them addressing each other as "Jacques." Madame Defarge now takes up her knitting and becomes absorbed in it, and the men are sent upstairs to the chamber they "wished to see."

After a brief but meaningful conference between Lorry and Defarge, the latter leads Lorry and Miss Manette quietly and secretly up a foul staircase, pausing only to kiss the hand of "the child of his old master," to a garret where Dr. Manette is kept behind a locked door. The three "Jacqueses" from the wine-shop are there peering at

Dr. Manette through some chinks in the wall. Monsieur Defarge says they are there for a good reason, these men who all share Monsieur Defarge's name, "Jacques," and he implies that an Englishman like Mr. Lorry would not understand. He sends them away, however, and opens the door, as Lucie Manette shudders and says, "I am afraid . . . of my father." There, in the dim light, "a white-haired man sat on a low bench, stooping forward and very busy, making shoes."

Commentary

Chapter 5 introduces the reader to the second of the "Two Cities," Paris, and to the incredible squalor and privation of the people. Oppressed by hunger, ignorance, poverty, and disease, a spilled cask of wine provides a moment of gaiety and happiness in the course of otherwise hopeless existences. It is significant here to compare the wild, frantic, almost animalistic scooping of the wine—dregs, mud, filth, and all—with the quiet satisfaction with which Mr. Jarvis Lorry drank his warming bottle of red claret before the coffee-room fire of the Royal George in Dover: the comparison is a striking one. In the poverty of Saint Antoine, there is no comfort, unless it is in the guarded knowledge that a time of vengeance is coming.

The tall, gaunt fellow who scrawls the word "BLOOD" on a wall is a grim specter used by Dickens to point forcefully toward the blood bath of the French Revolution that lies ahead. In reprimanding the fellow, Ernest Defarge "perhaps accidentally perhaps not" places his hand on the man's heart, while inquiring of him if there is no other place on which he might write such things besides public property. Defarge's concern is not for the defacement of public streets, but the touching of the man's heart signifies that such a vengeful word should be written, not publicly, but on one's heart—until the time arrives to make it public.

With the opening of Chapter 5, it is as if the reader is suddenly turned toward a stage illuminated and alive with action. The broken cask, the scurrying citizens of Saint Antoine, the grotesque and wine-smeared man and his delight in writing "BLOOD," the end of the laughter and dancing, and the return to quiet despair—it is as if stage lights were suddenly brightened for action and then lowered just as quickly. The effect is a dramatic one, and we already know of Dickens' great affection for the theater and of his natural inclination toward incorporating its dramatic effects and devices into his writing. This wine scene is a splendid example of Dickens' dramatic eye, his talent for staging, at its very best.

In describing the people of Saint Antoine as "gaunt scarecrows," Dickens is both literal and figurative in his language. Literally, they look like scarecrows; but figuratively, he is indulging in metaphor in suggesting such an appearance and, at the same time, referring to "the birds, fine in song and feather [who] took no warning." The implied comparison here is between fine, gay, beautifully plumed birds, heedless of the warning that the scarecrows provide, and the equally gay, heedless, and beautifully clothed French aristocrats. The strong comparison is one of several moments in the novel when Dickens' social commentary is couched in striking poetical language.

This chapter introduces Ernest and Therese Defarge. They are well-drawn characters in their own right, figures representative of the spirit, the fierce hate and longing for retribution that smoldered in France during the years before 1789. But they are more than this. They are leaders in the revolutionary movement, and will take a significant part in it. They are different than the unfeeling rabble of the streets. They are intelligent and cunning, particularly Madame Defarge, who will be seen to be the more forceful of the two. In the chapter that follows, it will be wise for the reader to draw a comparison between Defarge and his wife. They are alike in their hate of aristocratic oppression, but they are different in the intensity with which that hate manifests itself.

When Lucie, Jarvis Lorry, and Defarge arrive at the attic room where Dr. Manette is hidden away under lock and key, they discover the three customers from the wine-shop peering in at him through a chink in the wall. To Mr. Lorry's indignant question as to whether Defarge makes "a show of Monsieur Manette," Defarge replies that only a chosen few see him and that the sight is likely to do them good. Why should such a sight do anyone any good, the reader may wonder. Defarge allows his revolutionary associates, all conveniently named Jacques, to see the wretched and broken Dr. Manette as a reminder of what the brutality of the aristocrats and the agony of the Bastille can do to a man. The sight is a shocking one, and the lesson even stronger. When we at last see the bent figure, gray before his time, hunched pitifully over his shoemaker's bench, we can understand how a series of such sights all over France, real evidence of the people's suffering, could forever mark the spirit of hate and revenge on their hearts.

QUESTION: What is the significance of Madame Defarge's knitting? Why does Monsieur Defarge show Dr. Manette to a chosen few; and what does he mean when he says to Mr. Lorry, "Enough; you are English; that is another thing"?

CHAPTER 6

The Shoemaker

Summary
Dr. Manette works steadily at his shoemaking. He had a raggedly-cut white beard, a hollow face, and unusually bright eyes. He

is dressed in tattered rags. His physical and emotional state is that of a wasted, spiritless, unfeeling being, totally removed from reality. With great difficulty he answers the few questions Monsieur Defarge asks him, and he gives his name as "One Hundred and Five, North Tower." He does not recognize Mr. Lorry, but for just a moment, the faintest glimmer of recognition seems to cross his face when Mr. Lorry calls him by name and reminds him that Monsieur Defarge and he, Mr. Lorry, are old associates of his. Almost immediately, though, he relapses into his trance-like state. Eventually, Lucie approaches him and sits beside him, pityingly. Looking at her hair, he opens a folded rag tied around his neck by a string. It contains "one or two long golden hairs" which had been found when he was taken to prison where his daughter had laid her head upon his sleeve in leave-taking. "It is the same," he says wonderingly. "How can it be! When was it? How was it!"

At Lucie's insistence, Monsieur Defarge and Mr. Lorry quickly complete the preparations to transport the Manettes and Mr. Lorry to England that very night. The only other witness, besides Monsieur Defarge, to their departure from France in a coach is Madame Defarge who "leaned against the doorpost, knitting, and saw nothing." Monsieur Defarge, riding with them to the city gates, insures their safe departure with a whispered word or two to the guard at the gates.

Commentary

With Chapter 6, Book I of *A Tale of Two Cities* concludes. Dickens had led the reader from the mystery of the curious messages uttered on the Dover road to what appears to be a happy reunion of father and daughter after eighteen years of separation. As we shall see, that happiness can only be temporary. Ahead of Dr. Manette, his daughter, and their good friend, Jarvis Lorry, lies the French Revolution, an event that will draw these three people, and others we have not yet met, back to the Continent and a far different relationship with Monsieur and Madame Defarge.

We see Madame Defarge as the coach is making ready to leave and, here, Dickens underlines the mysterious aspect of this woman, subtly affirming that there is a depth and hardness to her that we have only begun to notice. In the last chapter, Ernest Defarge knelt and kissed the hand of Lucie Manette, daughter of the man for whom he had worked years ago. In the garret, he is firm yet tender and gentle with the feeble doctor, and had locked him in to prevent the bewildered man from coming to any harm. It is true that Dr. Manette is used as an object lesson to stir the memory and revolutionary heat of those that peer at him through the wall, but it is also true that Ernest Defarge sheltered him when he was removed from the Bastille.

Madame Defarge waits by the shop door as Dr. Manette is brought down. There was an "unnatural silence," and Madame, involved as usual with her knitting, "saw nothing." Dickens is very artful in his development of this shrewd woman's characterization. She sees nothing, and is apparently an unobserving bystander absorbed in her thoughts and her knitting. However, when Dr. Manette, who was now inside the coach, asked Jarvis Lorry, who was about to enter, for his shoemaker's tools, Madame Defarge heard him and went to fetch them. By such subtleties as this on Dickens' part, we can see that nothing escapes her eyes or her ears. In fact, she is the most observant of all. She appears to lack emotion, or at least to be an example of those Frenchmen and Frenchwomen so oppressed by the social conditions of pre-revolutionary France that all compassion had been stamped out—leaving only a smoldering, explosive hate.

The reader is probably aware of a growing suspicion, on his own part, about Madame Defarge. She is *too* quiet, *too* unobservant, *too* busy with her incessant knitting. She has yet to play her true role in the novel; and when she does it will be a powerful one, terrible and frightening for the Manettes and their friends. She is an example of strong characterization, created gradually, more by suggestion and the stirring of the reader's suspicions than by direct statement from Dickens or by any positive action on Madame Defarge's part.

QUESTION: What is the significance of "One Hundred and Five, North Tower"? Why is it relatively easy for Dr. Manette to escape from France?

Book II — The Golden Thread

CHAPTER 1

Five Years Later

Summary

It is 1780—five years after the Manettes left Paris. Tellson's Bank is "the triumphant perfection of inconvenience"—old-fashioned, ugly, incommodious—and proud of it. Also, Tellson's is actively involved in the unbelievably unjust laws of capital punishment, "a recipe much in vogue" at that time.

The scene shifts to the poor but well-kept apartment of Tellson's odd-job man, Jerry Cruncher. Upon waking, Jerry furiously throws his muddy boot at his wife who kneels praying in a corner, "flopping" as Jerry calls it. Despite his wife's protests that she prays *for* him, Jerry is convinced that she prays against him and their twelve-year-old son, and that is why he is plagued with bad luck.

Jerry and his son go to work, which consists of Jerry's sitting outside of Tellson's on a wooden stool, his son standing beside him, waiting for odd-jobs.

Commentary

Tellson's Bank, "the triumphant perfection of inconvenience," nevertheless represents a haven of stability and safety in these troubled times. The heavy piling up of detail on top of detail, exemplified by the description of Tellson's, is a typical Dickens trait. Although the *Tale* is only half as long as most of Dickens' novels and he, himself, chafed at the "incessant condensation," he cannot always control his tendency to "overwrite." (Whether the "overwriting" is a virtue or a fault is another matter.)

Dickens protested against capital punishment not only in this book and other books but in his own life as well. He wrote letters to the press and spoke out against capital punishment. In 1849, after attending some executions in London, he began, by writing to *The Times*, a movement that resulted in abolishing public hangings.

One of the primary reasons why Dickens' readers regard the *Tale* as the least Dickensian of all his novels is the absence of comic characters. Jerry Cruncher and, possibly, Miss Pross are the only characters reminiscent of the broadly drawn caricatures that figure so prominently in the novels prior to the *Tale*.

The name Jerry calls his wife on occasion—"Aggerawayter"—is simply his way of pronouncing "aggravater."

Amid the description of the Crunchers' daily life two notes of mystery are introduced. We are told that whereas Jerry Cruncher "often came home after banking hours with clean boots, he often got up next morning to find the same boots covered with clay," with his eyes red as from lack of sleep. And, at Tellson's with his father, young Jerry muses, "Al-ways rusty! His fingers is al-ways rusty! Where does my father get all that iron rust from? He don't get no iron rust here!"

QUESTION: How would you characterize Jerry Cruncher, his family, his home life?

CHAPTER 2

A Sight

Summary
Tellson's sends Jerry to Old Bailey to serve as a messenger for Mr. Lorry. Old Bailey is especially crowded today, for the spectators expect Charles Darnay, the "quiet and attentive" young man on trial, to be found guilty of treason and, therefore, sentenced to be drawn and quartered. This kind of spectacle is a real treat for the Londoners at Old Bailey. Two spectators in the courtroom, however, do not share the eager excitement of the motley crowd. They are the Manettes, father and daughter, the latter of whom can only regard the prisoner with terror and compassion. The prisoner looks at them so keenly that all eyes in the courtroom survey them. Jerry learns that the Manettes are witnesses against the prisoner.

Commentary
Dickens continues to paint a dire picture of eighteenth-century London. We find that spectators pay an admission fee to see the trials at Old Bailey, the criminal court at Newgate Prison, as they can pay to see the insane inmates at "Bedlam," a notorious asylum. The cruelty of the "law" is once again attacked by Dickens in this chapter. And we learn that judges, themselves, died from diseases caught from the miserable prisoners. In retrospect, however, the picture of London pales in the more hideous glare of the atrocities in France.

A critic once said that the most interesting thing about Charles Darnay is that he bears the same initials as Charles Dickens! Despite this parallel, it is Sydney Carton (whose name is not revealed in this chapter), with his hands in his pockets and his eyes on the ceiling, who seems closest to Dickens himself. Carton, who is not mentioned by name until Chapter 3, is probably the fullest and best drawn character in the novel. Dickens said, in writing a preface to this book, that he first conceived the idea for the Tale when he was acting in Wilkie Collins' drama The Frozen Deep. In that play, Dickens played the role of the self-sacrificing lover, the man who gave his life so that the woman he loved could have the man she loved. Dickens seems to identify with such martyred love. Many biographers and critics feel that largely because of the Ellen Ternan relationship and the isolation Dickens felt from his family, friends, and public at this period in his life, he identified most closely with Sydney Carton.

QUESTION: What passages reveal Dickens' strong satire?

CHAPTER 3

A Disappointment

Summary

Mr. Attorney-General, in a long-winded bombast, informs the jury that he can produce two witnesses—one, a former friend of Darnay and the other, Darnay's servant—who have secured evidence of Darnay's treason. Mr. Attorney-General will prove that for at least five years Charles Darnay, who has been a frequent traveller between France and England, has been supplying France with valuable information concerning the plans and movements of England (thereby aiding the American Revolution).

The first witness, John Barsad, appears in the witness box. The wigged gentleman sitting not far from Mr. Lorry (Mr. Stryver) cross-examines Barsad and goes a long way towards discrediting him. After the servant, Roger Cly, Mr. Lorry takes the stand. The attorney-general suggests that Darnay could have been one of the other two passengers on the mail coach to Dover that November night five years ago in 1775. Although Mr. Lorry insists he cannot be sure that Darnay was one of those passengers, he does relate that Darnay returned to England with him a few days later, boarding the packet ship at Calais a little after midnight.

Next, Miss Manette is forced to identify Darnay as the passenger on the packet ship that night and to relate, much to her discomfort, some seemingly incriminating evidence against him.

Dr. Manette is the next witness. He can only remember the prisoner's calling on him in his London home some three or three-and-a-half years ago. He painfully tells the court that his mind was a blank for some time and he remembers nothing of the trip from France to England five years ago.

Because of the strong resemblance between Charles Darnay and "a wigged gentleman" sitting nearby, which the gentleman (Sydney Carton) calls to the attention of Darnay's attorney in a note which he tosses to him, the testimony of the next witness is discredited. The witness cannot positively identify Charles Darnay as the man he saw five years ago who was supposedly giving information to the enemy. The man he thought was Darnay could have just as well been Carton—or anyone, for that matter.

After the jury withdraws to consider a verdict, Sydney Carton speaks briefly with Charles Darnay. He informs him that Miss Manette, who had swooned after her testimony, is feeling better now.

Charles Darnay is acquitted, and Jerry Cruncher is sent hurrying to report the verdict to Tellson's.

Commentary

This chapter lays especially significant groundwork as far as the plot is concerned. We should note that the prisoner's counsel (Mr. Stryver) discredits John Barsad by suggesting that Barsad is a spy in the pay of the English government. Roger Cly is also tainted with this spy accusation. Even more significant is the way in which Mr. Stryver expedites Darnay's acquittal. The striking resemblance between Sydney Carton and Darnay will determine the conclusion of the novel. We learn, too, that Darnay travels under an assumed name and that "delicate and difficult" business forces him to travel frequently between England and France.

Note how in this chapter, as in others, Dickens uses the human forehead as a means of expressing personal feelings and character. For example, we read that Lucie Manette's "forehead was painfully anxious and intent" as she gave her evidence, and that in the courtroom "a great majority of the foreheads there, might have been mirrors reflecting the witness."

QUESTION: What does Jerry mean when he says at the end of the chapter, "If you had sent the message, 'Recalled to Life,' again, I should have known what you meant this time"?

CHAPTER 4

Congratulatory

Summary

Dr. Manette, Lucie, Mr. Lorry, and Mr. Stryver congratulate Charles Darnay on his narrow escape from death. Dr. Manette who looks like a different man from the shoemaker in the Paris garret, suddenly lapses into a curious expression as he regards Darnay with "an intent look, deepening into a frown of dislike and distrust, not even unmixed with fear." He quickly shakes it off, though, and father and daughter go home.

Sydney Carton then makes his presence known and exchanges sharp words with Lorry about "the business mind." After Lorry departs, Carton takes Charles Darnay to a tavern where Darnay eats his dinner and Carton, not quite sober when he met Darnay, drinks still another bottle of wine. Carton says he would like to forget the world: "It has no good in it for me . . . nor I for it." After drinking a toast to Miss Manette, proposed by Darnay, Carton insolently informs

Darnay that he does not really like him. They part, however, "without ill-blood on either side," but with Carton saying that "I am a disappointed drudge, sir. I care for no man on earth and no man on earth cares for me." Left alone, Carton realizes that Darney represents everything Carton could have been, even to the blissful extent of winning Miss Manette's affections. He admits to himself that he hates Darnay. With that, he falls into a drunken stupor.

Commentary

We see Sydney Carton at his worst: insulting, baiting Darnay at every step, half-sober and half-drunk, lacking dignity and civilized restraint. Somehow, though, just as Dickens says later on that we are drawn to pestilence or the guillotine, we are drawn to Sydney Carton.

The death image at the end of the chapter—picturing Carton with "a long winding-sheet and the candle dripping down upon him"–is an obvious foreshadowing.

When Lorry calls, "Chair there!" he is requesting a sedan chair, an enclosed seat supported on poles by two bearers. It was somewhat the equivalent of today's taxicab.

QUESTION: What comparisons and contrasts can you make between Charles Darnay and Sydney Carton?

CHAPTER 5

The Jackal

Summary

Mr. Stryver and Sydney Carton are constant companions, both in drinking and in the court of law. Late the same night of Darnay's trial, on schedule, Carton goes to Stryver's lodgings. Stryver, the "lion," is "a glib man, and an unscrupulous and a ready, and a bold." He relaxes while Carton, the "jackal," works long and hard to extract the essence from a heap of statements which he then hands over to the waiting Stryver. Herein lies the answer to Mr. Stryver's steady climb up the ladder of success: Sydney Carton does much of his work for him. Carton is a man of great talent but he lacks the character traits that would make those talents work for his own advantage. From his earliest school days, he was the boy who "did exercises for other boys, and seldom did [his] own." Now that he is a man, he further dissipates himself with drink. However, "Stryver never had a case in hand, anywhere, but Carton was there, with his hands in his pockets, staring at the ceiling of the court."

When Stryver suggests that Carton was "quick to see what happened to the golden-haired doll [Lucie Manette]," Carton is annoyed. He denies that Lucie is pretty, and he leaves. As he walks into the depressing dawn of a lifeless day, Sydney Carton envisions a world of love and beauty that could be his if he would only work for it. But, sadly, he resigns himself to the "blight on him" and allows it to "eat him away."

Commentary

We gain more insight into Sydney Carton. If we haven't already surmised it, we know now that Sydney is a man of great ability but, unfortunately, he does not use it for his own good.

Mr. Stryver is probably drawn from Dickens' own experience. While Dickens was working on the *Tale*, he had, according to Edgar Johnson's *Charles Dickens*, occasion to see in action a certain Edwin James, "a pushing and unscrupulous barrister who was later debarred for malpractice. Dickens quietly observed his florid, hard-faced bluster; in the sixth and seventh numbers of *A Tale of Two Cities* he brought in the character of Mr. Stryver. . . . 'Stryver is a good likeness,' [Dickens' friend observed.] 'Not bad, I think,' [Dickens] agreed. 'Especially after only one sitting.'"

QUESTION: In what way is Sydney Carton a "jackal" to the "lion," Mr. Stryver?

CHAPTER 6

Hundreds of People

Summary

Dr. Manette, Lucie, and Miss Pross occupy two floors of a comfortable corner house near Soho Square. Dr. Manette practises his profession and earns just as much as he needs.

This fine Sunday, Mr. Lorry, who has become a close friend of the Manettes, is paying his usual weekly visit, but finds only Miss Pross at home. Miss Pross complains that too many people, unworthy of her "Ladybird" (Lucie), come seeking after her "to take Ladybird's affections away from [her]." Mr. Lorry astutely recognizes Miss Pross as "one of those unselfish creatures" who willingly dedicates herself to serving the youth and beauty of another, with never a thought of mercenary gain. Miss Pross says there is only one person worthy of her Ladybird and that is her brother, Solomon, "if he hadn't made a mistake in life." Mr. Lorry knows that the brother Miss Pross refers to so affectionately is a "heartless scoundrel who had stripped her of everything she possessed, as a stake to speculate with, and had abandoned her in her poverty for evermore, with no touch of compunction."

Mr. Lorry questions Miss Pross regarding the shoemaker's bench and tray of tools that have been brought from the garret in Saint

Antoine and now stand in Dr. Manette's bedroom. Mr. Lorry wonders if the doctor "has any theory of his own, preserved through all those years, relative to the cause of his being so oppressed; perhaps even to the name of his oppressor." Miss Pross says that Ladybird thinks he has, but Miss Pross believes he stays away from the subject because, having lost himself once before, he does not want to lose himself again. He is still obviously troubled, however, for sometimes he arises at night and paces back and forth for hours until Lucie's love and comfort restores him again.

Lucie and Dr. Manette arrive and soon they all sit down together to an excellent meal, expertly planned and supervised by Miss Pross. Later, they take their wine under the plane-tree. As each moment goes by, Mr. Lorry expects to see the "hundreds of people" that Miss Pross said come calling on Lucie. Only Charles Darnay appears, at which point Miss Pross is suddenly afflicted with "a fit of the jerks" and goes into the house.

In the course of conversation, Darnay relates a story he heard when he was imprisoned recently in the London Tower. Workmen found an old dungeon with the letters DIG inscribed on a wall. The floor under the inscription yielded some ashes of a paper and a small leather case or bag that some unknown prisoner apparently wanted to keep from the jailer. Dr. Manette reacts violently to this story, but he hastily insists he was startled only by the raindrops that have just begun to fall. Nevertheless, Mr. Lorry thinks he noticed the same intent, fearful expression cross Dr. Manette's face when he looked at Darnay as he had noticed four months ago in the passages of the court house.

Tea-time comes, and still no "hundreds of people"—only Sydney Carton.

With ominous foreshadowing, the peaceful Sunday at the Manettes' ends with a violent thunderstorm and a sound like thousands of footsteps echoing from the streets.

Commentary

Dickens introduces a symbol that he will continue to use in the novel—the symbol of the echoing footsteps. Although these sounds never directly materialize in London, the "hundreds of people" whom Miss Pross imagines—and whose footsteps Lucie sometimes fancies she hears—eventually materialize in the hordes of rebellious French peasants who will directly affect the peaceful little group that meets together this Sunday.

That Charles Darnay's story about the London Tower prisoner connects in some way with Dr. Manette is obvious. Dickens had definite feelings about this kind of foreshadowing as an artistic device. Wilkie Collins, a friend of Dickens and also a writer—especially of mysteries—was not satisfied with the way Dickens handled the plot of the *Tale*. Collins advocated the technique of "anticipation," very much in vogue at that time. He suggested, for example, that the complete story of Dr. Manette that Dickens reveals much later in the story be told earlier. In this way the reader's interest would be stimulated to follow closely the progression of the doctor's fate. Dickens, however, was opposed to such severity of technique. "Anticipation" would give away the story too early and all that would be left would be a mechanical working-out of what was already inevitable. Dickens wrote, "I think the business of art is to lay all that ground carefully, not with the care that conceals itself—to show, by a backward light, what everything has been working to—but only to *suggest*, until the fulfillment comes. These are the ways of Providence, of which ways all art is but a little imitation."

QUESTION: Why is Miss Pross afflicted with "a fit of the jerks" when Charles Darnay comes to visit? How many instances of foreshadowing can you find?

CHAPTER 7

Monseigneur in Town

Summary
Monseigneur, a member of the French court and the essence of the aristocratic class, requires four lavishly attired servants to serve him his morning chocolate. Monseigneur spends far more time on, and pays far more attention to, the Comedy and the Grand Opera than to the desperate needs of France. He has taken his sister from training in a convent and married her to a rich farmer-general, a very convenient marriage for Monseigneur who dearly needs someone to manage his affairs.

As always, Monseigneur's hotel (mansion) is the scene of a gay reception peopled by powdered, perfumed, brocaded aristocrats whose only care, besides the sheen of their satin breeches or the glitter of their jewels, is that they should remain in Monseigneur's favor. And so they bow and fawn and cringe before him. One man, the last to leave, offers a curse to the Monseigneur—"I'll devote you to the Devil!"—which the Monseigneur does not hear. This man is "about sixty, handsomely dressed, haughty in manner, and with a face like a fine mask." He boards his carriage and his coachman "drove as if he were charging an enemy," racing recklessly through the narrow streets of Paris. In Saint Antoine a small child is run down by the horses and killed. The Marquis tosses a gold coin to the grief-stricken father, Gaspard. He also tosses one to Defarge, after asking his name, who has philosophically tried to soothe the broken father. As the Marquis pulls away from the unpleasant scene, a coin flies into his carriage and rings on the floor.

Incensed, the Marquis orders the carriage stopped, but he sees nothing other than the grovelling father and a woman now standing beside him where Defarge had stood. She is knitting, but she alone of all the peasants there looks steadily at the Marquis' face.

Other carriages come rushing through and the peasants watch, like "rats . . . out of their holes," and the dark, stout woman "still knitted on with the steadfastness of Fate."

Commentary

The picture of decayed aristocracy that Dickens presents is a striking one, all the more so for the biting irony in the tone of his description. Dickens says that Monseigneur simply could not dispense with a single servant in the preparation and serving of his chocolate. The tone is bitterly sarcastic here, the same quality that we saw in the opening chapter of the book. It is a cruel but artificial world that Dickens describes for the reader, a world of highly refined grotesques, morally diseased, and all the more repulsive in its evil frailty when contrasted to the grimly realistic image of a peasant humanity withering and dying to preserve aristocratic self-indulgence. "The leprosy of unreality disfigured every human creature in attendance upon Monseigneur."

In this chapter we meet Monseigneur, the Marquis, as well as encountering once again Ernest and Therese Defarge. All four represent social types in Dickens' novel, but three continue in the narrative as individual characters. Monseigneur is a great lord, pampered and adored by fawners and influence seekers, while his self-indulgence and refinement have become extreme vices. He himself, as the representative of a class, is a social disease. The Marquis, in his desire for attention from Monseigneur, his annoyance at the lack of it, his haughty cruelty in the child's death, and concern only with the safety of his horses, is the epitome of the aristocrat that drove the French people to revolution and indiscriminate use of the guillotine. He is a social type, to be sure, but Dickens retains him in the narrative. He becomes, if only momentarily, an individual character. Ultimately, he affects the circle of friends that stood by the Manettes' window in London at the beginning of a rainstorm and heard prophetic echoes of footsteps that were to descend upon them.

The Defarges appear once again, representing that part of the people's spirit that has not been trampled into submission, a spirit that flares with hate for the aristocrats with every encounter. Madame Defarge particularly stands as the symbol of unyielding fate itself, silent and expressionless, an almost timeless figure as she knits without pause. However, the Defarges are supremely important characters in the book, and their encounter with the Marquis in the dirty streets of the Saint Antoine quarter of Paris is soon to bear violent fruit.

A "farmer-general" was a person who purchased from the government the privilege of collecting taxes in a district, keeping for himself all that was above the amount specified. The "wheel" was a cruel device of torture and punishment. Monseigneur's "hotel" refers here to his own private mansion.

QUESTION: Trace the way in which Dickens builds up your antagonism against the Marquis D'Evrémonde.

CHAPTER 8

Monseigneur in the Country

Summary

Riding towards his château, the Marquis passes through "a beautiful landscape" but one with evidence of scanty crops, and through the poor little village over which he is the lord. The people have been reduced to starvation primarily by the heavy taxes which are levied on almost everything. A village mender of roads informs the Marquis—whom the villagers call "Monseigneur"—that he saw a man hiding underneath the Marquis' carriage as it ascended the hill. The man was not of the local area, and had jumped off a short while back. The Marquis orders his official, Gabelle, to conduct a search for him.

Continuing homeward, the Marquis is stopped at a cemetery by a woman who pitifully petitions him for "a morsel of stone or wood" to be placed over her husband's grave so that, when she soon dies "of the same malady," the burial place will not be forgotten, as are the increasing number of other "heaps of poor grass." Ignoring her request, the Marquis quickly rides on to his château. There, he asks if a Monsieur Charles, whom he expects from England, has arrived. He has not.

Commentary

The crimson of the setting sun, reflected especially on the Marquis, ties in color-wise with the spilled wine of the broken cask in Book I, Chapter 5, and with the word "BLOOD" that Gaspard scrawled upon the wall. These images of "red" are everywhere in the novel and they all point in one direction: death. Especially ironic is the Marquis' comment as he glances at his red-steeped hands: "It will die out directly." Symbolic, too, as the carriage descends a hill, is "the sun and the Marquis going down together."

The manner in which the Marquis is lord over his village is a vestige of feudalism, the overthrowing of which was to be one of the major victories of the revolution.

In the village of the Marquis, two minor but important characters are introduced: the mender of roads and Gabelle. *Gabelle* is the French word for the detested salt-tax that the peasants were forced to pay.

Dickens picked up certain words and names from Carlyle's history and used them, often in a totally different context, in the *Tale*.

QUESTION: What details of setting and incident paint the clearest picture of the Marquis' village? Who is Monsieur Charles?

CHAPTER 9

The Gorgon's Head

Summary

Believing his expected guest will not arrive that night, the Marquis begins his sumptuous dinner alone. Once, he believes he sees something outside his window, but nothing is found. Then his guest arrives: his nephew, Charles Darnay, from London. It is clear from their conversation that although they are closely related through blood, they are worlds apart in their ideas and philosophies, and the nephew expresses doubt that the uncle would care to save him were he "to the utmost brink of death." He suggests that his uncle may even have helped surround him with "suspicious circumstances." The Marquis firmly believes in the system now in existence where the few wealthy aristocrats hold in total submission, through "fear and slavery," the majority of the population. Darnay, on the other hand, seeks "to execute the last request on [his] dear mother's lips, and obey the last look of [his] dear mother's eyes." That is, he wishes to show mercy and to redress the wrongs that his family has inflicted upon the peasants of France. Further, he renounces France and also the property, "the wilderness of misery and ruin," that he will inherit someday upon his uncle's death. The Marquis says, "I will die, perpetuating the system under which I have lived." Also, in a sinister fashion, he lets Darnay know that he knows about "the Doctor with the daughter" now in England.

The night passes and the day begins, just as they have always done, except for one slight difference: Monsieur the Marquis is dead, murdered in his bed with a knife through his heart. Around the knife is a note: "Drive him fast to his tomb. This, from Jacques."

Commentary

That death is inevitable is a recurrent theme in literature. Another way of dealing with this theme is to point out the inevitability of fate; fate being any circumstance beyond man's control. Greek literature frequently deals with this theme, often showing that fate, and especially death, controls the destiny of man. Dickens feels that the Marquis is largely an instrument of fate. Because his family has heaped abuse upon the people of France for two hundred years, the Marquis is fated to die. Therefore, to reinforce his point that fate and death are inevitable in the case of the Marquis, Dickens alludes quite frequently to Greek literature. The horse-drawn carriage, for example, is "attended by the furies" and the postilion's whip "twined snake-like about [the horses'] heads." The continual references to the mask-like face of the Marquis also derive from the Greeks. The actors in the ancient Greek theater always played behind masks and the masks of Greek drama—one happy and one tragic—are famous dramatic symbols. In this chapter, the "Gorgon's head" is drawn from Greek mythology. The Gorgon was a female monster, so hideous in appearance, that men who looked at her turned to stone. By the time we learn that the "mask" of the Marquis has joined the ranks of stone faces decorating the château, we know that fate has finally caught up with the Evrémondes.

Although not directly stated, the implication is clear that the Marquis was responsible for Charles Darnay's being accused of treason some months ago. We also learn that Darnay's name is really the same as the Marquis', Evrémonde, though that name has not yet been specified in the book.

QUESTION: Contrast the personalities and viewpoints of Charles Darnay and the Marquis. Why are they enemies?

CHAPTER 10

Two Promises

Summary
It is one year later (about 1782) and Charles Darnay is a successful teacher and translator of French in England. He is also deeply in love with Lucie Manette, unknown to her. In an interview with Dr. Manette, Charles confesses his great love for Lucie and swears never to consider separating father and daughter (if, indeed, he ever could) if he should be so lucky as to marry Lucie. Dr. Manette promises that if Lucie ever speaks affectionately of Charles, he (the doctor) will tell her of Charles' love for her and will not speak against him. The doctor continues by saying that if the man Lucie loves has any offences against him whatsoever, they would all be obliterated for Lucie's sake. He refuses to listen further when Charles tries to tell him his real name and why he is in England. The doctor makes Charles promise to tell him only on the morning of his marriage.

That evening, when Lucie returns home, she hears her father working at his shoemaker's bench. He came when she called "and they walked up and down together for a long time."

Commentary
Dickens' attempts to strengthen the characterization of Charles

Darnay do not add much substance to what we already know. It follows naturally that Darnay pursues the only occupation he knows, that of a French teacher and translator. It is also perfectly logical for him to have fallen in love with the beautiful and kind-hearted Lucie Manette. The only point about which we cannot be sure, and which intrigues us, is Dr. Manette's reticence towards him. The psychological thinness of the novel is probably most evident in Charles Darnay. He presents no idiosyncracies, no bigger-than-life faults or virtues to catch our fancy. He is kind, considerate, unselfish, courteous, self-possessed—all in all, quite bland and colorless.

Dr. Manette's turning to his shoemaking tools when he is troubled has an interesting source. Carlyle's history tells how the French king, Louis XVI, often deeply involved in government problems which he had neither the ability nor the desire to solve, escaped from his troubles with the tools of a locksmith, finding a happy outlet in working with his hands.

QUESTION: What is the significance of Dr. Manette's reaction to Charles' declaration of love?

CHAPTER 11

A Companion Picture

Summary

Late the same night, Sydney Carton is finishing a large quantity of work for Mr. Stryver. Mr. Stryver confides to him that he intends to do Miss Manette the great service of marrying her. Sydney seems barely to respond, but he drinks a newly made punch "at a great rate." Stryver urges him to marry someone with a little property, someone to take care of him "against a rainy day."

Commentary

Mr. Stryver, who bullies and "shoulders" his way ahead in life, continually empties Sydney Carton's keen legal mind in exchange for a few bowls of alcoholic punch. It is interesting to note the persistence of Stryver in criticizing and belittling Carton on every occasion—as well as Carton's apparent disregard for his companion's insulting condescension. The psychological situation here is a curious one. Stryver knows that Carton has the superior legal mind, and is not above rummaging it. His continual scolding and reprimanding of Carton for social lapses, and for what Stryver sees as an insensitive soul, is actually a compensation in his own mind that crowds out his unethical use of Carton's skill. To inflate a host of Carton's faults, and seeming faults, is to minimize Carton's ability. This also makes Stryver's own professional stature appear less tainted, ethically, in his own eyes and by his own standards makes him emerge as the finer of the two men. Stryver is a stuffy, supercilious prig, but is keenly aware that Carton is essential to him. Therefore, his endless tirade of assaults on the man is actually a necessary rationalization for him.

The question arises as to why Sydney Carton endures Mr. Stryver's abuse. There are several reasons. His alcoholism and Stryver's constant feeding of it helps him to tolerate his offensive associate. However, Carton fully realizes his own wretchedness, and maintains an attitude of constant and wearying defeatism. Certainly, he is not impressed with Stryver's presumptuous, blustering, and patronizing ways. He is even amused by them. Yet, to endure so much belittling from so obnoxious a fellow is to suggest perhaps that Carton, even unconsciously, wishes to hear in Stryver's stupid, pompous criticisms the echoes of his own self-condemnation.

QUESTION: In what sense is the title of this chapter ironic?

CHAPTER 12

The Fellow of Delicacy

Summary

Mr. Stryver, on his way to the Manettes' to propose to Lucie, stops in at Tellson's to tell Mr. Lorry of Lucie's good fortune. Mr. Lorry advises Stryver not to go on "such an object without having some cause to believe that [he] should succeed," and suggests that he (Lorry) sound out Lucie first that evening and then call on Stryver to tell him the result. Stryver cannot understand how Lucie can possibly refuse him, and is angered by Lorry's belief that she would, but he agrees to Mr. Lorry's plan. When Lorry calls on him that night to report the outcome—that he would, indeed, not be successful in his proposal—Stryver acts nonchalant and declares that the loss is most certainly the Manettes' and not his.

Commentary

Some readers may be disappointed at the outcome of this chapter. They would prefer having Mr. Stryver let down forcefully by Lucie herself. A man of such inflated ego and aggravating pomposity needs a stronger "comeuppance" than Mr. Lorry gives him. It would probably be difficult, however, and certainly out of character for Lucie, all sweetness and light, who never hurt anyone, to suddenly acquire the spirit and revulsion that the situation demands.

QUESTION: Why does Mr. Stryver believe Mr. Lorry? Will he simply forget about the rebuff?

CHAPTER 13

The Fellow of No Delicacy

Summary

Sydney Carton, who, in addition to being a frequent visitor at the Manettes, has been haunting the streets surrounding the Manette home, calls on Lucie and declares his love for her. At the same time, he insists on his own unworthiness and that he will become worse. He asks nothing more than for Lucie to remember always how deeply he cares for her and that he would make "any sacrifice for you and for those dear to you." The tragic baring of his soul had brought tears to his eyes and to hers. After assuring her that he will never refer to this matter again, he departs, saying "Farewell! God bless you!"

Commentary

It is said that Sydney Carton holds a position in literature no less illustrious than Shakespeare's Hamlet in his appeal as a tragic hero. He is also compared to Heathcliff in *Wuthering Heights*. He belongs to that great gallery of torture-racked heroes whose capacity for pain and love captivates the reader's total sympathies. Women, especially, adore him. They see in him all the potential that the love of a woman can sometimes bring to fruition.

QUESTION: Why does Sydney Carton have more appeal than Mr. Stryver—or Charles Darnay? If Lucie had loved him instead of Charles Darnay, do you think she could have saved him?

CHAPTER 14

The Honest Tradesman

Summary

As Jerry Cruncher sits on his stool outside of Tellson's one day, an unusual funeral procession comes down Fleet Street. At his son's "Hooroar!" when he learns it's a funeral, Jerry boxes the boy's ears soundly. The crowd around the hearse and mourning coach loudly voices its objections: "Yah! Spies! Tst! Yaha! Spies!" The solitary mourner escapes, and the crowd pours into, over, and around the mourning coach and directs the hearse to the burial ground. Jerry learns that this is the funeral of Roger Cly, the servant who had testified against Charles Darnay at the Old Bailey trial over a year ago, and he joins the mob. The mob has its way with the burial and, finally, after several hours of terrorizing and destruction, disperse. Jerry, meanwhile, meditates on the corpse: ". . . he was a young 'un and a straight made 'un.'' On his way back to Tellson's, he pays a short visit to his medical adviser, a distinguished surgeon.

After spending an evening at home keeping his wife from praying or meditating against him, Jerry arms himself with a sack, a crowbar, a rope and chain, and other "fishing tackle," and at one a.m. goes out into the night. Unknown to his father, young Jerry follows him. Along the way, Jerry picks up two companions and the three of them, followed by young Jerry, make their way to a church graveyard. When young Jerry sees that their "fishing" yields up a coffin, he takes off and keeps running until, half dead, he reaches his home.

Young Jerry is awakened at daybreak by the noise of his father beating his mother, blaming her again for opposing his "honest trade.'' The boy senses "something had gone wrong.'' Finally, big Jerry goes to sleep, and so does his son.

On their way to work that morning, young Jerry slyly asks his father: "What's a Resurrection-Man?" Upon his father's agreeing that a Resurrection-Man's "goods" are "persons' bodies," young Jerry declares that he "should so like to be a Resurrection-Man when I'm quite growed up!" This secretly pleases his father.

Commentary

The crowd scene that opens this chapter is only a mild prelude to the crowd scenes we shall encounter later in Paris. Dickens always reacted violently to crowds. Many of his novels, especially his only other historical novel, *Barnaby Rudge*, deal just as graphically with mob destructiveness. Far from being democratically inclined, Dickens believed in a capitalistic form of government in which the capitalist (like the regenerated Scrooge, for example) takes a kindly interest in the populace and treats them generously. Dickens' novel, *American Notes* (1842), based on his travels in America, deals harshly with America and the American way of life. We should note, too, however, that one of the primary targets for his unfavorable comments was the institution of slavery.

Jerry's interest in funerals, in general, and Roger Cly's, in particular, is carefully planted.

Later, we shall learn why Jerry is in a particularly bad mood this morning.

Despite its grisly nature, this is one of this book's few chapters in which touches of Dickens' famous humor are evident.

QUESTION: What are some of the humorous touches in this chapter? Might the chapter title be considered humorous in any sense?

CHAPTER 15

Knitting

Summary

At six o'clock in the morning, in Defarge's wine-shop, people are already gathered and some are drinking. At noon, Monsieur Defarge and the mender of roads from the village of the late Marquis enter, dusty and thirsty, having walked a day and a half. Gradually, three of the men leave, one by one, and soon Monsieur Defarge and his new-found friend leave to go up to the garret where Dr. Manette once worked at his shoemaker's bench. Already in the room are the three other "Jacques"—the ones who had left the shop singly, and who are the same three that Defarge had allowed to look through the chink at Dr. Manette. At the command from Jacques Four (Monsieur Defarge), Jacques Five (the mender of the roads) tells his oft-repeated story of how he saw a man hiding underneath the Marquis' coach the evening of the night that the Marquis was murdered, a year ago. As his tale unfolds, we learn that this man was Gaspard, the father of the child who was killed under the wheels of the Marquis' coach. After a year in hiding, Gaspard was finally found and brought to the Marquis' village and imprisoned there. Monsieur Defarge had presented a petition to the king and queen, stating that the man was understandably grief-stricken to the point of insanity because of the cruel and senseless death of his child. Nevertheless, the man was hanged, forty feet above the village fountain, and was left dangling there, casting a pall over the entire village.

The four Jacqueses dismiss Jacques Five and vow that "the château and all the race" must be listed in their register, "doomed to destruction." Their register, in which everything is recorded, is Madame Defarge's knitting: "Knitted, in her stitches and her own symbols. . . . It would be easier for the weakest poltroon that lives, to erase himself from existence, than to erase one letter of his name or crimes from the knitted register of Madame Defarge."

Monsieur and Madame Defarge later take the mender of roads to Versailles to see the procession of the king and queen and members of their court. His vociferous adoration of the bejewelled splendor pleases the Defarges. Monsieur Defarge says that such a man gives the aristocrats a false sense of security: "Then, they are the more insolent, and it is the nearer ended." Madame Defarge, reassured by the mender of roads that he would "pluck . . . to pieces" the richest and gayest dolls in a heap and "strip the feathers" from the finest birds in a flock unable to fly, for his own advantage, tells him, "You have seen both dolls and birds to-day." Then he is sent home.

Commentary

Certain details now fall into place. We learn the unfortunate fate of Gaspard and, very important, the significance of Madame Defarge's constant knitting. It is true that the peasant women of France sat at the foot of the guillotine and nonchalantly knitted while the heads rolled from under the blade, but the whole concept of Madame Defarge's knitted register is Dickens' own. Among other details of French dress and customs of the time, we find that wooden shoes were worn.

QUESTION: What does Madame Defarge mean when she speaks to the mender of roads about the "dolls" and the "birds"?

CHAPTER 16

Still Knitting

Summary

The mender of roads returns to the village of the dead Marquis, and the Defarges return to Saint Antoine. Monsieur Defarge learns from an ally, "Jacques of the police," that another spy has been commissioned for their quarter—an Englishman, John Barsad. Madame Defarge makes a point to memorize the man's name and physical description so that she can "register" it.

When Defarge expresses weariness at the slow progress being made, Madame Defarge assures her husband that "vengeance and retribution require a long time," but they are coming.

The following noon a stranger comes into the wine-shop. Casually, Madame Defarge pins a rose in her headdress and with that action, just as casually, "the customers ceased talking, and began gradually to drop out of the wine-shop." The stranger, whom Madame Defarge instantly recognizes and carefully registers in her knitting, is John Barsad. He plies her with questions, but is rewarded with no incriminating answers. When Monsieur Defarge enters the shop, Barsad greets him with an engaging "Good day, Jacques," but Monsieur Defarge responds only by stating that his name is Ernest. Next, the spy informs Defarge that he knows Defarge had harbored Doctor Manette some time ago and he relates the entire circumstances of Dr. Manette's being removed to England. Barsad then informs them that Miss Manette is going to be married to the nephew of the Marquis whom "poor Gaspard" had murdered.

This information makes a strong impact, especially on Monsieur Defarge. He fervently hopes that destiny will keep Miss Manette's husband—Charles Darnay—out of France, for his name is now registered alongside John Barsad's in Madame Defarge's knitting.

That evening, Madame Defarge makes her rounds among the

women of the village. They sit this night as they do every night—knitting, knitting, knitting. The day is not far off when they will be "knitting, knitting, counting dropping heads."

Commentary

The reader recalls that John Barsad is the "friend" of Charles Darnay who testified against him at the Old Bailey trial over a year ago. Barsad, first a spy for the English throne and now a spy for the French throne, becomes an increasingly important character.

We see the contrast between Monsieur and Madame Defarge: she is by far the deadlier of the two. Her hardness and grim determination are an important prelude to the news that Charles Darnay is the nephew of Monsieur the Marquis. When she registers Darnay's name next to John Barsad's, we know that nothing will stop her from taking her revenge.

In this chapter, seemingly unrelated elements introduced into the book earlier begin to intertwine and we see their relationships to the main plot.

QUESTION: What details prove that the peasants are working together as a group?

CHAPTER 17

One Night

Summary

It is the night before Lucie's marriage to Charles Darnay. She and her father sit alone under the plane-tree. Dr. Manette confides to Lucie some of the dreams he had when he was a prisoner. Even in his most glorious dreams, he tells her, he never achieved the love and happiness that Lucie has given him in actuality. Lucie passionately declares her undying love for him and vows that her love will continue to flourish even though she is getting married. She and Charles will live in the upper rooms of the Manette house, and life on the quiet corner in Soho will continue to be filled with love and contentment.

Commentary

In this chapter, as he does elsewhere in the novel, Dickens tries to show what it is like to be imprisoned. The whole gamut of imprisonment—trials, prisons, prisoners, executions—shows up frequently in Dickens' novels. When Dickens was twelve years old, his father was imprisoned for debt at Marshalsea, and the whole Dickens family, excluding Charles, went to live with him there. Charles was confined in a prison of a different nature. He lived alone in a slum boarding house and worked in a grim blacking warehouse. For almost a year he lived under these desperate and squalid conditions. The whole episode must have left a deep impression on the heretofore sheltered, upper-middle-class boy. *Little Dorritt* describes the infamous Marshalsea prison; *Sketches by Boz*, his first book, tells how he gazed at Newgate prison with "mingled feelings of awe and respect," and it describes a condemned man's last night alive. In *American Notes*, Dickens wonders what solitary confinement is like in a Philadelphia jail; and one of the high points of *Barnaby Rudge* concerns the burning of Newgate prison.

Some critics and biographers feel that the exceptionally tender and romantic scene in this chapter springs from Dickens' feelings for Ellen Ternan. He was old enough to be her father and, in order to compensate for a somewhat unrealistic love affair, perhaps, he romanticized it as the inseparable union between father and daughter.

QUESTION: Do you think Lucie is wrong to marry? How does Dr. Manette assure her that she is doing the right thing?

CHAPTER 18

Nine Days

Summary

Lucie, Mr. Lorry, and Miss Pross wait outside the room where the bridegroom, Charles Darnay, is having a conference with Dr. Manette. Mr. Lorry promises Lucie that he and Miss Pross will take excellent care of the doctor during the next two weeks while she and Charles are honeymooning, following which the doctor will join them in a two-week trip to Wales. Affectionately, he kisses her with "an old-fashioned bachelor blessing." When the doctor and Charles emerge from the room, Mr. Lorry observes that the doctor is "deadly pale." Though his composure seems unaltered, Mr. Lorry sees that some of the "old air of avoidance and dread had lately passed over him, like a cold wind."

Charles and Lucie are happily married, quietly and privately in a church. Upon their departure, Dr. Manette goes to his shoemaker's bench and, losing all sense of his true identity, works feverishly at his shoemaking. Mr. Lorry, for the first time in his life, takes time off from Tellson's and stays with the doctor. For nine days Mr. Lorry and Miss Pross try their best to return Dr. Manette to his real self, but to no avail. His mind is far removed from the present; his hands are "growing dreadfully skilful" at his shoemaking.

Commentary

Dickens' intent to maintain the suspense of the novel is nowhere more evident than in this chapter. Our curiosity is building: what strange event in Dr. Manette's past links him so dreadfully to Charles Darnay?

QUESTION: Do you approve of Mr. Lorry and Miss Pross keeping from Lucie the pitiful relapse of Dr. Manette? Is there any evidence that he will come out of it this time?

CHAPTER 19

An Opinion

Summary

On the morning of the tenth day, Mr. Lorry awakens to find the shoemaker's bench and tools put aside and Dr. Manette his old, real self again, though without recollection of the past nine days. The episode is not referred to until after breakfast, when Mr. Lorry questions the doctor about a "friend" of his who had suffered a prolonged and profound shock, who was gradually restored to his original keenness of mind and body, but who suffered a slight relapse. It becomes clear that the doctor knows who the "friend" is that Mr. Lorry is describing, and he thoughtfully continues the conversation, seeking details.

Dr. Manette informs Mr. Lorry that some strong revival of old thoughts and remembrances that were the original cause of the sickness must have triggered the relapse. The doctor says, further, that he thinks the worst is over and the "friend" is unlikely to suffer any renewals of the disorder. Mr. Lorry urges the doctor to consent to the removal of the tangible evidence of the old way of life. Although he is obviously referring to the shoemaker's bench and tools, he speaks of a blacksmith's forge. The doctor struggles within himself. Such an occupation represented a welcome haven during those terrible days of imprisonment, and the idea that sometime in the future "he might need that old employment, and not find it, gives him a sudden sense of terror," he says. Finally, he agrees.

When the fortnight since Lucie's wedding passes, Dr. Manette leaves to join her and Charles for a holiday. That night, Mr. Lorry and Miss Pross, feeling "like accomplices in a horrible crime," destroy the shoemaker's bench and tools.

Commentary

Mr. Lorry's method of telling the doctor about the past nine days is reminiscent of a much earlier episode when Lorry informed Lucie that her father was still alive. This technique of approaching a difficult truth through the indirectness of third-person narrative seems to be consistent with Mr. Lorry's personality. Here is another example of the tact and diplomacy that he has built up over the years as a "confidential bachelor clerk" at Tellson's. This kind of indirectness can also be construed as a Victorian trait. The twentieth century often brands the so-called "good taste" and "inoffensiveness" of the Victorians—and, especially, of the Victorian novels—as hypocritical, maudlin, and unrealistic. Whether we respect or reject Victorian style is a matter of personal preference. We may think that the two men in this chapter project a quiet dignity, perfectly appropriate under the circumstances; or we may think that the scene is unrealistic because of too much human kindness.

QUESTION: What does Dr. Manette really believe caused his relapse? Why do Mr. Lorry and Miss Pross destroy the shoemaker equipment?

CHAPTER 20

A Plea

Summary
The first person to appear to offer his congratulations when Mr. and Mrs. Charles Darnay arrive home is Sydney Carton. Taking Darnay aside, Carton apologizes for having been "insufferable about liking you, and not liking you" on the earlier occasion when he was unusually drunk. He asks Charles if they can be friends, and if he may have the privilege of visiting the house whenever he wishes. Charles consents and the two men shake hands.

That night, Lucie begs her husband never to speak slightingly of Sydney Carton, and asks him to believe that Carton has a heart, though seldom revealed, "and that there are deep wounds in it. . . . I have seen it bleeding." She also says, "I am sure that he is capable of good things, gentle things, even magnanimous things." Charles is captivated by her "sweet compassion."

Commentary
The relationship between Lucie and Charles is clearly one of deep trust and adoration. Despite his own unsuccessful marriage, or perhaps *because* of it, Dickens could always idealize the love between a man and a woman, and find within this love life's regenerative force. He is never optimistic about the general state of society: witness the brutality of the mobs and the endless cycle of wrongs begetting wrongs, seen especially in the Reign of Terror following the immediate outbreak of the French Revolution. He believes that the source of salvation lies within the individual.

One of the chief criticisms directed against the *Tale* is that the two themes of love and revolution do not merge. The regeneration that springs from the love theme in the novel—the love between father and daughter, husband and wife, friend and friend—weaves one thread in the story (the Golden Thread) that does not interweave with the other theme of revolution. The love theme, confined to only a few individuals, never affects the Defarges, the revenge, the guillotine, in fact, none of the scenes both in England and in France that reveal the other side of man's nature. Dickens seems to say, further, that an unbridgeable gulf separates the individual from society, for the day of "a beautiful city and a brilliant people rising from this abyss," which Sydney Carton envisions at the end of the novel, will take "long years to come."

QUESTION: Describe the relationship between Charles Darnay and Sydney Carton. What scene is Lucie referring to when she says, "I have seen it bleeding"? Why does Carton seek free access to the Darnay house?

CHAPTER 21

Echoing Footsteps

Summary

As the years pass, Lucie continues to weave the golden thread that binds together in love and happiness all who live in and frequent the house on the corner in Soho. Lucie and Charles have a beautiful daughter, and then a son. The son, however, dies. Sydney Carton "claimed his privilege of coming in uninvited" at most six times a year, but the children show a fondness toward him. He continues to serve as Mr. Stryver's "jackal," and Mr. Stryver adds to his already established prosperity by marrying a widow with property and three boys.

It is now mid-July (July 14), 1789, and Mr. Lorry arrives at the Manette-Darnay household, hot and tired. There is such uneasiness in Paris that Tellson's customers over there are transferring their property to the London Tellson's as fast as they can. They sit and listen to the echoes of "numerous and very loud" footsteps.

The scene shifts to Saint Antoine in Paris where, at this very moment, footsteps are raging. The peasants are arming themselves with every kind of weapon imaginable, centering around Defarge's shop. Defarge shouts "Patriots and friends, we are ready! The Bastille!" With a roar that overflows all of France they march on the Bastille. Hour upon hour they storm the massive stone walls and the eight great towers. Finally, the Bastille surrenders. Defarge grabs one of the prison officers and demands to be shown One Hundred and Five, North Tower. In the cell, he finds two initials scratched in the wall—"A.M." for Alexandre Manette, and the words "a poor physician." He and

Jacques Three search for anything hidden, Defarge even groping "with a cautious touch" up the chimney.

The mad and roaring ocean of revenge-starved peasants continues to rise. They hack to death the governor who had defended the Bastille and shot the people. Madame Defarge completes the job by hewing off his head with her knife. They hoist up one of the governor's soldiers on the ropes where previously only lamps have hung. The sea of vengeance rolls madly on: "The loudly echoing footsteps of Saint Antoine escort through the Paris streets . . . Heaven defeat the fancy of Lucie Darnay, and keep these feet far out of her life!"

Commentary

A great deal of the description of the storming of the Bastille Dickens borrowed directly from Carlyle. For example, Dickens' passage reads: ". . . the living sea rose, wave on wave, depth on depth, and overflowed the city to that point. Alarm-bells ringing, drums beating, the sea raging and thundering on its new beach, the attack begun . . ." Carlyle's passage reads: ". . . behold . . . how the multitude flows on, welling through every street; tocsin furiously pealing, all drums beating the *générale*: the Suburb Saint-Antoine rolling hitherward wholly, as one man!" Dickens catches not only many of Carlyle's details, but also his furiously paced prose style.

The role of the women during the siege also comes from Carlyle. He devoted eleven chapters of his history to "The Insurrection of the Women," and one of his female leaders was Demoiselle Theroigne. Later, in Carlyle's account, Demoiselle Theroigne cries: "Vengeance, Victoire ou la mort!" Dickens named Madame Defarge's chief lieutenant The Vengeance, as we find in Chapter 22.

We should note the tremendous sympathy that the peasants feel for the prisoners. This will clarify later the intense appeal Dr. Manette has for the peasants as a former prisoner of the Bastille.

Defarge's groping in the chimney will have considerable significance later in the story.

QUESTION: Which details strike you as most vivid in the storming of the Bastille?

CHAPTER 22

The Sea Still Rises

Summary

One week after the storming of the Bastille, Saint Antoine learns from Monsieur Defarge that their detested enemy, Foulon, whom they thought dead, is alive, a prisoner at the Hôtel de Ville. This man, a government official, had once told the starving peasants that if they did not have food, they should eat grass. They march on the Hôtel, seize Foulon, drag him mercilessly through the streets, and hoist him up on the ropes. Soon they put his head on a pike and stuff his mouth with grass. Later in the day they hear that Foulon's son-in-law, another enemy, is being brought into Paris under cavalry guard. Saint Antoine seizes him, too, and sets his head and heart on pikes. "At last it is come, my dear!" Defarge says to his wife after they return home. "Eh, well!" she replies. "Almost."

Commentary

Atrocity piles up on top of atrocity. Because the *Tale* was serialized week by week in Dickens' new magazine and he desperately wanted the magazines to sell, he felt the pressure of making each new chapter exciting and suspenseful. The Foulon episode is a grisly one but no grislier than the chamber of horrors that Carlyle documents in his history.

"Hôtel de Ville" refers to the city hall, where administrative offices and a jail were located.

QUESTION: What is it that has "almost" come? In what manner does Dickens build up to its arrival?

CHAPTER 23

Fire Rises

Summary

In the starving village of the dead Marquis, changes are taking place, as they are in many villages throughout France. Among these are strange faces of low caste which appear, and just such an appearance occurs this day. As the mender of roads plies his trade, an unkempt, weary stranger approaches him, and the two "Jacqueses" greet each other. The stranger drops something into his pipe that blazes and then disappears in a puff of smoke. "Tonight?" asks the mender of roads. "Tonight . . . here." The stranger requests directions to an unnamed place, then says he will sleep by the road and asks the road-mender to waken him. This he does.

As night approaches and then deepens, the villagers meet and whisper together, instead of going to their beds. Monsieur Gabelle, the chief functionary, becomes uneasy. At the château of the dead Marquis, four mysterious, unkempt figures meet and set fire to the château. In the village, the mender of roads and two hundred and fifty friends note grimly that the pillar of fire "must be forty feet high." A rider from the château can enlist no aid, not from Monsieur Gabelle nor from the officers and soldiers stationed at the prison. The "four fierce figures trudged away, East, West, North, and South . . . towards their next destination.''

The villagers surround the house of Monsieur Gabelle, but he is able to escape, at least temporarily, by waiting out the night on his house top behind his stack of chimneys. Monsieur Gabelle is more fortunate this night than many of his fellow functionaries in other villages who are hoisted up on ropes and pulleys. Many other villagers and townspeople, too, are less fortunate than the mender of roads and his friends, for functionaries and soldiers were able to turn successfully and string them up. Fire continues. Where and when it all will stop, nobody knows.

Commentary

The terror continues. The firing of châteaux owned by aristocrats was a familiar sight in that awful time.

Significantly, Gabelle is saved. This is an important thread in the plot, as we shall see.

QUESTION: What is the full significance of the ''four, unkempt figures''? Why can the rider from the château solicit no aid from any quarter?

CHAPTER 24

Drawn To the Loadstone Rock

Summary

It is now 1792. Three years of tempest in France and peace in the Manette-Darnay household have passed. People like the Monseigneur in France have taken to their noble heels and fled. The entire court is gone. The king and queen have been removed from Versailles and taken to Paris where they are confined in the Tuileries palace. (In August, 1792, they are imprisoned in the Temple.)

Tellson's Bank in London has become the news center and gathering place for the displaced French nobility and for all those who are interested for one reason or another in the whereabouts and welfare of their French brethren.

Charles Darnay tries to discourage Mr. Lorry from making a business trip to Tellson's office in Paris. Darnay says that if *anyone* should make a trip to Paris, he himself should, because he, as a native Frenchman and one who has left property to the people there, might influence the French to exercise some restraint. Mr. Lorry points out the danger of Charles' going to France, and the necessity for his own going, which he says is the least he can do for his employer who has taken care of him for sixty years. And so he is going, accompanied by a bodyguard, Jerry Cruncher.

Monseigneur—the Frenchmen in Tellson's—and Mr. Stryver, along with many other Frenchmen and Britishers, continually speak of the Revolution as if there were no cause for it. Stryver speaks loudly of exteriminating all the rebels. Such talk makes Charles Darnay restless and uneasy.

While Darnay is with Mr. Lorry, a soiled, unopened letter is handed to the latter, and he is asked if he has yet found any information about the person to whom it is urgently addressed. Darnay sees that it is addressed to "the Marquis St. Evrémonde, of France"—his own real name. The secret of his name, imparted to Dr. Manette on the morning of Darnay's marriage, was to be kept inviolate between them, unless the doctor disclosed the truth. Not even Lucie knew her husband's real identity. Unsuccessful in the past in locating the missing Marquis, Lorry again shows the name to the French aristocrats in the bank. They do not know the whereabouts of the "nephew . . . of the polished Marquis who was murdered," but they do know something of his attitude and behavior. They disparage him and express hope that the "ruffian herd" in France will "recompense him . . . as he deserves." As Stryver, too, denunciates the lost Marquis, Darnay says that he knows the fellow, and Lorry gives him the letter to deliver. Alone, Darnay reads it.

The letter is from Gabelle who writes that he is in prison and will surely be killed if Monsieur (Darnay) does not come to Paris and clarify his case. He is accused of treason against the people. They will not believe that, acting upon Darnay's (the "emigrant's") instructions. Gabelle has wiped clean the slate of back taxes and has collected no rent on the Marquis' estate. They only know that Gabelle supervised the aristocratic estate and that there is no "emigrant" present to vouch for the leniencies that Gabelle says he allowed. He begs Darnay to come to his rescue, "for the love of heaven, of justice, of generosity, of the honour of your noble name." Darnay berates himself for having neglected his responsibilities in France these past years.

Through Mr. Lorry, who leaves for Paris that night, he sends the message to Gabelle "that he has received the letter, and will come." Mr. Lorry remains innocent of who "he" is. Darnay writes two letters of farewell, one to Lucie and one to Doctor Manette. The next evening he, too, leaves for Paris.

Commentary

Dickens makes the point that people do not learn from their mistakes. The aristocrats, both English and French, do not understand, or want to understand, the causes of the French Revolution. Stryver, above all, represents the bigotry and ignorance that often fatally determine the course of history. *A Tale of Two Cities* sounds a clear warning to Englishmen that they cannot continue to oppress the laboring classes with foul prisons, infamous charitable and educational institutions, poor working conditions, without the inevitable, vicious retribution.

In 1867, Dickens was sorely tempted to go to America to perform his famous readings. Financially, it was a golden opportunity. His health was becoming so bad, however, and he was so weary and depressed that his friends urged him not to go. He wrote: "I began to feel myself drawn towards America as Darnay in the *Tale of Two Cities* was attracted to the Loadstone Rock, Paris"—and he made the tour. It proved to be a "killing odyssey." Dickens suffered from a severe cold that became worse and worse, his leg was afflicted so that he could hardly walk, and he lost all appetite. He was not so fortunate as his hero, Charles Darnay. The "Loadstone Rock" clearly hastened Dickens' death, unlike his more fortunate fictional counterpart who was able to escape. Originally, the Loadstone Rock was a mythical rock that magnetically drew ships to it, where they crashed.

QUESTION: Why does Charles feel he has to return to Paris? Do you agree with him?

Book III—The Track of a Storm

CHAPTER 1

In Secret

Summary

Charles Darnay's journey to Paris is taking much longer than he anticipated. Not only do bad roads, bad equipment and bad horses delay him, but he is stopped continually by citizen-patriots stationed at every gate and taxing-house. For days he travels through France and he is still a long way from Paris. Finally, sleeping at an inn one night, he is rudely awakened and forced to accept and pay for two citizen-escorts who will ride with him into Paris.

At Beauvais, Charles faces a hostile mob shouting "Down with the emigrant!" In vain Charles tries to convince them he is in France of his own free will and that he is not a traitor. They speak of a decree, saying that his life is forfeit to the people. Charles learns from the postmaster, who finally helps him find safety, that a decree was passed on the very day he left England for selling the property of emigrants. Furthermore, there will be more decrees, if there are not already, that will banish emigrants and condemn to death all who return.

Charles' travels finally bring him and his escorts to the wall of Paris. Charles is very much affronted when an authority there refers to him as "this prisoner." Before long he is conducted into a guard room by this man, whom an officer addresses as "Citizen Defarge." The officer asks Charles a few questions, confirming his identity as "the emigrant Evrémonde," and tells him, "You are consigned to the prison of La Force."

Escorting Charles to the prison, Defarge questions him and gets confirmation that Charles is Lucie Manette's husband. Despite an obvious interest in Charles, Defarge declines his plea for "a little help," and when Charles asks Defarge if he can get a message to Mr. Lorry informing him of his imprisonment, Defarge refuses. Charles learns that the king is in prison, and he observes the terrible change that has infected Paris. He realizes his danger now but he cannot foresee the hideous blood-bath that lies ahead.

Charles is led into a chamber in the prison where many other prisoners of aristocratic heritage and breeding are housed. When they learn that he is "in secret," they grieve for him. Soon the jailer leads him into a small, solitary cell where Charles paces to and fro, in an unsuccessful attempt to keep his mind off the horrible memories of Dr. Manette's imprisonment.

Commentary

So begins the infamous Reign of Terror in which "eleven hundred" prisoners (according to Dickens) are slain. Many as innocent of crime against the French people as Charles Darnay are loaded into tumbrils and taken off to the guillotine; some are butchered before they get there. The murder of Charles' uncle, the Marquis, probably struck us as just retribution, considering the type of aristocrat he was, but the proposed execution of Charles Darnay, also a French aristocrat, is quite another matter. Dickens reveals the excesses of mob rule and, at this point, the downtrodden masses become the villains of the novel.

QUESTION: Why is Darnay imprisoned? What is running through his mind as he paces his cell at the end of the chapter?

CHAPTER 2

The Grindstone

Summary

Tellson's Bank in Paris is quartered in a wing of what was formerly the aristocratic mansion of the Monseigneur for whom four servants had made chocolate (Book II, Chapter 7). The French "patriots" have taken possession of the mansion, one of the chief attractions of which is a large grindstone standing in the courtyard.

Mr. Lorry is quartered in the bank section of the mansion, thinking to himself, "Thank God that no one near and dear to me is in this dreadful town to-night," when he is startled by the sudden appearance of unexpected visitors—Lucie and Dr. Manette, along with little Lucie and Miss Pross. They have come to Paris to retrieve Charles. Lorry is shocked to learn that Charles is in the maddened city.

Shortly after, a horrible scene is enacted outside in the courtyard. Forty or fifty men and women, smeared with blood and dangling pieces of linen and lace torn from the clothing of aristocrats, sharpen their red-stained and dripping weapons at the grindstone. "They are murdering the prisoners," Mr. Lorry whispers to Dr. Manette.

At Lorry's urging, Dr. Manette goes out into the courtyard. Because he had once been a prisoner in the Bastille, the patriots give him a rousing ovation and promise help for his kinsman, Evrémonde. The doctor leaves with the mob to secure Charles' release.

As the long night passes, Mr. Lorry gazes pityingly upon the stupefied Lucie and Miss Pross who is taking charge of little Lucie. At daybreak, the red sun comes up on "the great grindstone, Earth." The smaller grindstone stands permanently stained with red.

Commentary

One of the most horrifying scenes in the novel, this chapter is one of the many that capture the fury and violence of the French Revolution. The *Tale* may lack the individual characterizations that first brought Dickens fame, but it portrays brilliantly in mood and setting man's inhumanity to man.

The "Gazette" was a publication of the British government that contained notices including bankruptcies.

QUESTION: What will happen to Charles, Lucie, and the doctor in Paris?

CHAPTER 3

The Shadow

Summary
Mr. Lorry is upset because he is putting Tellson's in jeopardy by sheltering there the wife of an emigrant. He manages to find lodgings near the bank for Lucie and Miss Pross, and he stations Jerry Cruncher there as a bodyguard.

That night, Citizen Defarge comes to Mr. Lorry's room. He has a message from Charles to deliver to Lucie. Mr. Lorry leads him to Lucie's new-found lodgings. Madame Defarge—who has been knitting, as she was when Lorry last saw her seventeen years before—and The Vengeance accompany them. Madame Defarge looks hard at Lucie, little Lucie, and Miss Pross. A certain strange coldness in the Defarge becomes apparent. It worries Lorry. Lucie pleads with Madame Defarge as a wife and a mother to help her husband. Madame Defarge coldly replies that no one ever took pity on all of the wives and mothers she has known. With that she leaves, knitting again.

Mr. Lorry, although deeply troubled himself, tries to comfort Lucie.

Commentary
Madame Defarge represents, more than any other single character in the book, the hatred and the vengeance that inevitably assert themselves. Dickens often refers to her as Fate: her knitting, her finger, her fury acquire proportions larger than themselves. In her fanatical single-mindedness, she is more a symbol than a person, a symbol of the inevitable consequence of oppression.

QUESTION: Why does Madame Defarge want to see Lucie and, especially, the child?

CHAPTER 4

Calm in Storm

Summary
The horrible atrocities are kept secret from Lucie, especially the grotesque popularity of "the sharp female called La Guillotine." Dr. Manette communicates with Mr. Lorry, informing him of the progress, or, rather, the lack of progress, in the case of Charles Darney. Charles has been tried before "a self-appointed tribunal" but, just as it seemed he was about to be released, he was, due to an unknown cause, ordered held in the prison.

As the months wear on, Dr. Manette's determination to secure Charles' release and his fortitude in administering medically to all the varied and suffering humanity who throng Paris in these frightful times prove him to be a man of great strength. His Bastille imprisonment, formerly only a hideous nightmare, now serves a worthwhile end. The Revolutionists regard him with respect and awe. But the blood-bath rages on; the king is beheaded.

One year and three months pass, and Darnay is still a prisoner at La Force.

Commentary
Dickens' descriptions of the anarchy raging throughout France and, especially, his satiric treatment of "La Guillotine" and the "Samson" who works it take on a savagery seldom equalled in literature. But unlike many twentieth-century novelists who deny the existence of God in the wake of human brutality, Dickens testifies to his religious belief. Where the Cross is denied, he says, the guillotine takes its place, and the executioner tears away the gates of God's own temple every day. If we still doubt Dickens' basic religious and moral sense, the conclusion of the novel will verify his belief in the Eternal and in the basic morality of good triumphing over evil.

QUESTION: Why is it that the atrocities that Dr. Manette witnesses do not cause him to have a relapse?

CHAPTER 5

The Wood-Sawyer

Summary
Still under the banner "Liberty, Equality, Fraternity, or Death," the Revolutionists continue to feed the guillotine daily with victims taken from every social and economic stratum in France.

Lucie does her best to make a comfortable home and carry on the routine of daily life in their Paris lodgings, but underneath it all she grieves deeply. One day her father tells her that if she stands at a certain place during a certain time of day, Charles may be able to see her from a prison window. She must give no indication of her purpose. From then on, Lucie appears at the designated time and place, never missing a day. In the street where she stands lives a woodcutter who was once a mender of roads. He is very curious about why she comes and speaks to her each day. One day, using his saw as a "Little Guillotine," he lightly executes a "family" made of wood.

As Lucie, together with little Lucie, stands in her accustomed place, she witnesses a terrible scene. It is the Carmagnole. Some five hundred peasants—among whom are the woodcutter and The Vengeance together—dance a wild, frenzied, demon-like dance that frightens Lucie until the doctor appears to comfort her. He says Charles will be looking out the window, and she sends tearful kisses toward the tower. As she does, Madame Defarge passes them with a brief greeting and walks on, "like a shadow."

Dr. Manette tells Lucie that Charles will appear before the tribunal tomorrow. The doctor assures her that he has everything under control and that Charles will be a free man in a few hours.

Dr. Manette goes to see Mr. Lorry. There is someone with Mr. Lorry, someone who must not be seen.

Commentary

Another coincidence weaves its way into the plot: the woodsawyer who lives in the vicinity of La Force is none other than the former mender of roads. One of the chief criticisms directed against *A Tale of Two Cities* is that Dickens depends too heavily on coincidence. Charles Darnay's history just happens to link with Dr. Manette's history; Monsieur Defarge, besides being the leader of the *Jacquerie,* just happens to be Dr. Manette's former servant; and he just happens to marry the woman whose history also links with Charles Darnay's. And, when we learn who Mr. Lorry's new visitor is, we may wonder if anything more than coincidence brings him to Paris at this time. Jerry Cruncher's body-snatching weaves into the finished design, as do Roger Cly and John Barsad. Just about all of the main and supporting characters somehow interrelate with each other, often by striking coincidence. It is really only in retrospect, however, that we realize all this.

First Carlyle and then Dickens immortalized the ferocious dance of the Revolutionists— the *Carmagnole.*

QUESTION: What attitude does Dickens take towards the Revolutionists (the wood-sawyer and the five hundred dancers) in this chapter? How do you know?

CHAPTER 6

Triumph

Summary

Charles is brought before the dread tribunal. Among the spectators are Citizen and Citizeness Defarge. Neither look at Charles, but "they seemed to be waiting for something." At first, the rowdy, bloodthirsty populace screams for the emigrant's head. As soon as Charles reveals, however, that he married Alexandre Manette's daughter, their attitude abruptly changes and they shout for Charles' release. However, the trial continues. Charles and his two witnesses—Gabelle and Dr. Manette—confirm his story that he has always acted for the good of the French people and that he returned to France on the noble mission of exonerating Citizen Gabelle. Dr. Manette testifies furthermore that Charles, so far from being in favor with the aristocratic government in Englnd, was tried by it as the foe of England and friend of the United States. This is all the jury wants to hear. They vote him free.

In wild jubilation, the crowd—with the Defarges not among them—carries Charles to the lodging where he is passionately reunited with his family.

Commentary

This chapter prepares us for the awful turn of events about to come. The all-but-invisible line that separates triumph from tragedy casts an ominous shadow over Charles' victory. Dickens never lets us forget how, with the same jubilance, the mob that celebrates Charles' release today can chop off his head tomorrow.

QUESTION: What role have the Defarges played in securing Charles' release?

CHAPTER 7

A Knock at the Door

Summary

Although it is true that her father has saved Charles, Lucie feels "a vague but heavy fear."

Lucie and her family have been living frugally in Paris. Jerry does most of their servant-work. Each day, Miss Pross and Jerry venture forth to do the necessary marketing.

Suddenly, late in the afternoon of the day of Charles' release, four citizens come to arrest him. In answer to Dr. Manette's queries as to why Charles is arrested again, they say that "he is denounced—and gravely—by the Citizen and Citizeness Defarge. And by one other"—whose name they will not reveal.

Commentary

Charles' short-lived victory abruptly ends. As the revenge of Madame Defarge closes in, the lives of the two principal sets of characters from the two cities of the title will cross for the last time.

QUESTION: Who is the "one other" that has denounced Charles?

CHAPTER 8

A Hand at Cards

Summary

On their marketing expedition, "happily unconscious" of Charles' new danger, Miss Pross and Jerry go into a wine-shop to buy some wine. There, Miss Pross suffers a profound shock. She looks right into the face of her brother Solomon whom she has not seen for many years. Solomon does not want her to reveal his English identity. He insists he is French now, an official of the Republic. His whole attitude towards his weeping sister is harsh and cold.

After concentrating on Solomon for some time, Jerry finally recognizes him as the "spy-witness" against Charles at the Old Bailey trial years ago. At just this moment, Sydney Carton steps into the scene and completes the identification by supplying the name—Barsad. The reader learns now that Sydney was the unidentified character with Mr. Lorry at the end of Chapter 5. He has come to Paris to see if he can be useful in any way.

Now he informs Miss Pross and Jerry that Barsad is a "sheep of the prisons"—a spy under the jailers—and that he saw him leaving the prison of the Conciergie just an hour ago. He tells Barsad he wants to talk with him and firmly suggests that they go together to the office at Tellson's Bank. They leave Miss Pross and the three of them—Carton, Barsad (or Pross), and Cruncher—go to Tellson's.

First, Sydney helps Mr. Lorry recall who Barsad is. Then, he tells Lorry the bad news of Charles' second arrest. Commenting on the desperation of the times and the desperate stakes, Sydney proposes a plan. He downs a glass of brandy and then reveals, step by step, each piece of damaging evidence that he holds against Barsad. First, the French would not be pleased to learn that Barsad is really an Englishman. Second, Barsad, "formerly in the employ of the aristocratic English government, the enemy of France and freedom," might very well still be.

Barsad uneasily thinks over all this information with which

Carton can denounce him. Furthermore, Barsad knows there is even more damaging evidence against him that Carton does not know. For example, he had been a spy for the overthrown French government and he had spied on Saint Antoine and Defarge's wine-shop. He was sure, too, that he was registered in Madame Defarge's knitting and, upon Carton's denunciation of him, Madame Defarge would produce against him the "fatal register" and the blade would fall.

Carton continues to stack the deck against Barsad. Aided by Jerry Cruncher's testimony that Roger Cly's coffin had only stones and earth in it, Carton forces Barsad to admit that his supposedly dead English friend, Roger Cly, is actually his fellow "French" spy. That Barsad, a former English spy but pretending to be French, is in league with another former English spy who has feigned to have died will sound to the patriots like "a plot in the prisons, of the foreigner against the Republic," remarks Carton.

Barsad admits defeat and asks Carton what he wants from him. After making sure that Barsad can come and go in the prison when he chooses, Carton takes him into another room for "one final word alone."

Commentary

Many threads of the plot are beginning to interweave. The identity of Barsad and his tie-in with the principal characters, the relevance of Roger Cly's funeral and Jerry Cruncher's escapade that night all tighten the plot and, incidentally, reveal Dickens' remarkable inventiveness.

QUESTION: Sydney Carton is becoming an increasingly important character. He will, in fact, dominate the remainder of the novel. In what ways does this chapter reveal his growing importance to the novel?

CHAPTER 9

The Game Made

Summary

While Sydney Carton and Barsad are in the adjoining room, Jerry spends a few very uncomfortable minutes alone with Mr. Lorry. Lorry is angry that Jerry has been using Tellson's as a blind to carry on the disreputable business of body-snatching. Jerry pleads his cause saying that the medical doctors who buy the corpses are equally to blame, and that by banking their large accounts in Tellson's, they, too, are imposing on Tellson's. He continues with arguments so convincing and sincere, even promising to be a "regular digger" (a gravedigger) from now on and to "dig 'em in" so well that they will have to be safe, that Mr. Lorry says he may yet remain his friend.

Carton and Barsad return from the adjoining room, Carton saying that Barsad has nothing to fear from him now that their arrangements are made. When Lorry and Carton are alone, Mr. Lorry asks him what arrangements he has made. Sydney replies that if things go ill with Charles, he has ensured access to him, once. Mr. Lorry is disappointed. Carton asks that nothing be said to Lucie about these arrangements.

Mr. Lorry and Sydney Carton hold a touching conversation, full of sentiment and reminiscence. Lorry says his business for Tellson's is finished and he should soon leave Paris. Then, Mr. Lorry goes to visit Lucie. Sydney spends the night walking through Paris. First, he follows Lucie's route to the prison and visits the spot where Lucie stood every day outside of the prison, and he talks for a minute with the wood-sawyer there. Then, he stops at a chemist's shop and buys some small packets, which the shopkeeper warns him not to mix. As Sydney walks through Paris this night, a refrain keeps running through his head, a refrain that he remembers from his father's graveside service: "I am the resurrection and the life. . . ."

When morning comes, Sydney goes to the trial where Charles Evrémonde, called Darnay, is being tried for the second time in two days. His denouncers are Ernest Defarge, Therese Defarge and—Alexandre Manette! With the pronouncement of the last name a great uproar sweeps over the court. Dr. Manette immediately protests, insisting that his daughter's husband is dearer to him than his own life.

Citizen Defarge takes the stand. He testifies that on the day they stormed the Bastille he went to cell One Hundred and Five, North Tower, once occupied by Dr. Manette. There he found hidden in a hole a paper written by Dr. Manette's hand. The order is given: "Let it be read."

Commentary

Jerry Cruncher emerges as a genuine Dickensian character. His comical yet shrewd oration, in which he rationalizes his former body-snatching occupation, is one of the few instances in the novel where Dickens gives full rein to the talent that made him famous. Through his own dialogue Jerry reveals his shrewd insight into the double standards that society accepts. Why condemn the resurrection man for stealing and irreverence when the highly respected men of medicine and men of the cloth benefit even more than Jerry from the business of body-snatching? ("For you cannot sarse the goose and not the gander.") Despite his former abuses against his "decent wife," Jerry remains a sympathetic character. Not only has he proved himself a loyal and invaluable friend but, in this dialogue, his resolution for the future to "dig 'em in" instead of digging them out strikes with comic force, especially when he explains: "A man don't see all this here a goin' on dreadful round him, in the way of Subjects without heads, dear me, plentiful enough fur to bring the price down to porterage and hardly that, without havin' his serious thoughts of things."

The resurrection theme sounds more clearly than ever as Sydney Carton wanders through Paris. Many "recalled to life" sub-themes have presented themselves thus far in the novel: Dr. Manette's rehabilitation; Charles Darnay's two (so far) escapes from death; grotesquely, Jerry Cruncher's resurrection activities; Roger Cly's miraculous recovery; and Solomon Pross' reappearance. The concept of resurrection, as it relates to Sydney Carton, however, is the one towards which all the others have been pointing.

QUESTION: What details concerning Sydney Carton, his thoughts and his activities, build your suspense?

CHAPTER 10

The Substance of the Shadow

Summary
In 1767, in his "doleful cell" in the Bastille, after ten years of imprisonment, Dr. Manette wrote a long, detailed narrative describing the tragic experience that led to his imprisonment. The paper lay where he had hidden it in the wall of his chimney until Monsieur Defarge discovered it on the day the peasants stormed the Bastille. The paper tells the following story.

One night in December, 1757, two men, looking very much alike, ordered Dr. Manette into their carriage and took him to their home where a beautiful young woman lay very ill and delirious. Dr. Manette observed the letter "E" on a scarf that bound her arms. In her delirium she shrieked with the ceaseless regularity of a pendulum: "My husband, my father, and my brother!" Then she counted to twelve and said "Hush!" After giving her some medicine, the doctor was taken to a loft room over a stable, where he found another patient, a handsome young peasant boy, dying of a sword-wound. Before he died, however, he told the doctor the whole tragic story of his sister (the dying woman), his family, and himself.

His family were tenants of the twin brothers who had brought the doctor here to their home. These brothers of the aristocracy forced their tenants to work and live under insufferable conditions. His sister married an ailing young man, but was only married a few weeks when one of the brothers decided he wanted her. The two brothers then waged a cruel campaign to persuade the girl's husband to "lend" her to them. They harnessed him to a cart and drove him. They kept him outside all night to quiet the frogs and the next day put him back in harness again. But he was not persuaded. Taken out of his harness one day at noon, "he sobbed twelve times, once for every stroke of the bell, and died on her bosom." Still, the "younger" brother took her away, even though she was pregnant.

When the young boy told his father, his father's heart "burst." The boy took his other, younger, sister away, then returned and tracked the brother, forced him to draw his sword, and was thus fatally wounded. Just before he died, the boy drew a cross of blood in the air to signify that the Marquis and his brother and their "bad race" would some day have to pay for their crimes.

The brothers tried to make Dr. Manette promise that he would never tell what he knew about them. After a week the girl died. The doctor refused the "rouleau of gold" that the brothers gave him, but the next morning it was left at his door.

Dr. Manette decided to write what he had seen and send it to the minister. Before he could send the letter, he was visited by a beautiful but sickly woman who presented herself as "the wife of the Marquis St. Evrémonde." The doctor realized this man was the "elder" of the two brothers whom he had so recently seen. Wanting desperately to make some amends for her husband's and brother-in-law's inhumanity, she asked Dr. Manette for the name and address of the younger sister of the two dead young peasants so that she could help the girl. Dr. Manette, however, did not have this information. As the woman was ready to leave, the doctor saw a young boy in her carriage, her son Charles. She told the doctor that for this boy's sake she wanted to make amends. She feared that someday Charles would suffer for the Evrémonde sins, and says, "I will make it the first charge of his life to bestow, with the compassion and lamenting of his dead mother, on this injured family, if the sister can be discovered."

The same day Dr. Manette delivered his letter to the minister. That night, the doctor's servant, young Ernest Defarge, admitted a man who led the doctor into a trap. He was seized, identified by the two evil brothers who then burned the letter in front of his face, and was imprisoned in the Bastille.

If the Evrémondes had only sent news of the doctor's beloved wife sometimes during those awful first ten years in the Bastille, he might have felt that they had some spark of decency left in them. But now he believed that they were a totally cursed race and he denounced "them and their descendants, to the last of their race . . . to the times when all these things shall be answered for. I denounce them to Heaven and to earth."

When the reading of the letter was completed "a terrible sound arose" in the court, a clamoring for vengeance. "Save him now, my Doctor, save him!" smirks Madame Defarge.

The vote in the tribunal was unanimous: death to the accursed Charles Evrémonde, called Darnay, within twenty-four hours.

Commentary

Dickens' friend and biographer, John Forster, objected to the feudal atrocities practised by the Marquis and his brother upon their tenants in this chapter on the grounds that by the mid-eighteenth century such feudal excesses had died out. In reply to this objection Dickens wrote:

> I had of course full knowledge of the formal surrender of the feudal privileges, but these had been bitterly felt quite as near to the time of the Revolution as the doctor's narrative, which you will remember dates long before the Terror. With the slang of the new philosophy on the one side, it was surely not unreasonable or unallowable, on the other, to suppose a nobleman wedded to the cruel ideas, and representing the time going out as his nephew represents the time coming in. If there be anything certain on earth, I take it that the condition of the French peasant generally at that day was intolerable. No later inquiries or provings by figures will hold water against the tremendous testimony of men living at the time. There is a curious book printed at Amsterdam, written to make out no case whatever, and tiresome enough in its literal dictionary-like minuteness; scattered up and down the pages of which is full authority for my marquis. This is Mercier's *Tableau de Paris*.

The *Tableau de Paris* that Dickens refers to was among the two cartloads of books dealing with the French Revolution that Carlyle had delivered to Dickens' doorstep when Dickens asked for help with his proposed *Tale*.

A letter reprinted in Carlyle's history particularly intrigued Dickens. Found in the paper archives of the Bastille at the time of its fall and dated October 7, 1752, it reads:

> If for my consolation Monseigneur would grant me, for the sake of God and the Most Blessed Trinity, that I could have news of my dear wife; were it only her name on a card, to show she is alive! It were the greatest consolation I could receive; and I should forever bless the greatness of Monseigneur.

From this bit of inspiration Dickens conceived the device for revealing the secret behind Dr. Manette's imprisonment and for returning Charles Darnay to prison.

QUESTION: How much of the mystery surrounding the relationship between Dr. Manette and Charles Darnay is now resolved? What further major revelations do you suspect may come?

CHAPTER 11

Dusk

Summary

After the court adjourns, Charles and Lucie are granted a parting embrace. Though she acts bravely, she tells him "that this will break my heart" and that she shall soon join him in death. To Dr. Manette, who is crushed, Charles offers his love and understanding for the doctor's acceptance of him as his daughter's husband, even after he discovered Charles' real identity. Lucie watches, comfortingly, as Charles is led away. Then she collapses at her father's feet. Sydney Carton advances from a corner and tenderly carries her to a coach, and then into her own rooms. There, little Lucie begs him to "do something to help mamma, something to save papa!" He kisses the child.

Carton urges Dr. Manette to again exert his influence in Charles' behalf. The doctor assures him he will try every means possible, and promises to report at Mr. Lorry's later that evening. As Lorry and Carton part, they appear to agree that "there is no real hope" of saving Charles.

Commentary

As Sydney Carton kisses little Lucie he murmurs words that only she hears: "A life you love." This reveals much about his present plans when the reader recalls that in Book II, Chapter 13, in ending his profession of love for Lucie, but his unworthiness of her, he said, "think now and then that there is a man who would give his life, to keep a life you love beside you!"

QUESTION: Both Mr. Lorry and Carton apparently agree that "he will perish; there is no real hope." Why, then, does Carton insist upon Dr. Manette's doing everything possible to save Charles?

CHAPTER 12

Darkness

Summary

After leaving the Manettes', Carton pauses in the street. "Shall I do well . . . to show myself?" he wonders. Then he decides, "I think so. It is best that these people should know there is such a man as I here. . . ." He turns toward Saint Antoine. Stopping to slightly alter the arrangement of his clothing and his hair, he finds his way to the Defarge wine-shop. There, pretending to be an Englishman who understands little French, he overhears a conversation among the

Defarges, The Vengeance, and Jacques Three. First, they remark about how closely he resembles Evrémonde. Soon, when Defarge indicates that he is perhaps not wholeheartedly for Darnay going to the guillotine, Madame Defarge vehemently explains to The Vengeance and Jacques Three why she is so determined to exterminate Charles Darnay and anyone connected with his family: she is the younger daughter in the peasant family that was so cruelly mistreated by the Evrémonde brothers, as described in Dr. Manette's paper. It is her responsibility to avenge those crimes, she asserts.

Making his way to Lorry's, Carton and Lorry wait for Dr. Manette until after midnight. Finally the doctor appears. "The instant he entered the room, it was plain that all was lost." He has relapsed into his shoemaker-identity, and fretting pitifully because he cannot find his bench. Carton and Lorry are dismayed. Sydney places into Mr. Lorry's safekeeping two certificates—one with his own name on it, the other for Lucie, her child, and the doctor—which will enable them to leave Paris safely. Sydney impresses upon Lorry that grave danger confronts Dr. Manette and his family if they remain in Paris, for Madame Defarge is preparing to denounce them. Lorry promises to see that Lucie, her child and father start from Paris the following afternoon, Lucie being told that it was "her husband's last arrangement" for them to do so. Carton says he will join them. "The moment I come to you, take me in, and drive away."

Helping Lorry take the mindless doctor to Lucie's, Carton pauses for a moment outside the house. "He breathed a blessing towards it and a Farewell."

Commentary

Dickens does not explicitly state why Carton feels "that these people should know there is such a man as I here." The implication is clear, however, that if the Revolutionists know an Englishman named Sydney Carton resembles Charles Darnay, it will be helpful in the plan Carton has in mind, though we can yet only suspect what that may be.

A final thread falls into place as the reason for the intensity of Madame Defarge's revenge is revealed. The careful plot that has so ingeniously interwoven the lives of the characters in both cities is reaching its conclusion.

QUESTION: To what extent does Sydney Carton's visit to the wine-shop advance the plot?

CHAPTER 13

Fifty-two

Summary

In the dark prison, Charles Darnay tries to resign himself to his impending execution, knowing that "on his quiet fortitude" depends much of his dear ones' future peace of mind. He writes three letters: one to Lucie, one to Dr. Manette, and one to Mr. Lorry. He does not think of Carton.

The following day he listens as a distant clock strikes away the hours. When two hours remain before his execution, Sydney Carton is secretly admitted to the cell by Barsad, who remains concealed. Carton forces Charles to change clothes with him and then dictates a letter for Charles to write to Lucie. Unknown to Charles, it repeats Sydney's words of long ago in which he expressed his desire to be of service to her and her loved ones. While Charles writes, Sydney passes a capsule near his nose which soon renders Charles unconscious. Barsad, who knows about the exchange, calls two prison guards to help him remove the man who swooned during the visit to his friend who is about to be executed. Carton is left alone, awaiting the execution intended for Charles.

Among the fifty-two prisoners who are to be executed that day is a pitiable young seamstress who recognizes that Sydney is not "Citizen Evrémonde." "Are you dying for him?" she whispers. To his affirmative reply, she says, "O you will let me hold your brave hand, stranger?" Carton answers, "Yes, my poor sister; to the last."

Meanwhile, the coach carrying Dr. Manette and his family and Mr. Lorry—including the still-unconscious figure of "Sydney Carton"—is making its slow and fearful way toward freedom.

Commentary

Symbolism asserts itself strongly in this chapter. The title and the number of prisoners (fifty-two), Charles Darnay's rightful name (Evrémonde) and the image of the blood running into "the boundless everlasting sea" combine to present a tragic view of human affairs. Evrémonde is a clear if unfounded and unlinguistic play on Everyman. Thus, guilty or not, every man is condemned to die every week of every year in endless succession.

Dickens' abrupt transition to first person plural at the end of this chapter offers fascinating speculation. First, it can be just a device to involve the reader more directly in the exciting escape from France. Second, it can also be a warning from one Englishman to all Englishmen: "Look out, look out, and see if we are pursued. The wind is rushing after us, and the clouds are flying after us, and the moon is plunging after us, and the whole wild night is in pursuit of us, but so far we are pursued by nothing else." So far. So far only the cosmos is seeking revenge. But if we Englishmen continue to abuse our masses, if we do not immediately institute governmental and social reforms, we too can suffer a revolution, every bit as bloody and as horrifying as the French Revolution described in this novel.

In this chapter we learn why Carton had stopped at a chemist's shop in Book III, Chapter 8.

QUESTION: Why does Dickens make it necessary for Sydney Carton to drug Charles Darnay in order to effect Darnay's escape.

CHAPTER 14

The Knitting Done

Summary

As the events of the previous chapter are taking place, Madame Defarge meets with The Vengeance and Jacques Three in the shed of the wood-sawyer (the former mender of roads). She reiterates her determination to exterminate the Evrémondes, Lucie and her daughter being her primary targets after Charles. She does not trust her husband to know her plans because he has relented toward the doctor. The wood-sawyer is to testify in court that Lucie, during her long watches outside the prison, was signalling—"clearly plots." The doctor will similarly be denounced for the same reason. The group plans to meet that night in Saint Antoine to inform against their victims.

Then, seeking to catch Lucie at home in a grieving state, awaiting her husband's execution, in a state of mind that will make her liable to further compound her guilt against the Republic, Madame Defarge walks towards Lucie's house. She is "a tigress . . . absolutely without pity. If she had ever had the virtue in her, it had quite gone out of her."

Miss Pross and Jerry Cruncher had been left behind when the coach carrying the others had left. They were to leave shortly after in a light conveyance, overtake the coach, and go ahead of it to make arrangements that would facilitate the passage of the others. Jerry vows "never no more" to do "it" (body-snatching) and "never no more" to interfere with Mrs. Cruncher's "flopping." He adds, "I only hope with all my heart as Mrs. Cruncher may be flopping at the present time." Jerry leaves to get their vehicle and pick up Miss Pross near "the great cathedral door."

As Miss Pross readies herself to leave, Madame Defarge confronts her in the apartment asking to see "the wife of Evrémonde." The two women stand their ground, neither one budging from her stand, one trying to hide the fact of Lucie's flight and to protect Lucie, the other to attack her. They clash bodily. During the struggle, Madame Defarge's pistol discharges and kills her.

Miss Pross hastens through the streets of Paris in time to meet Jerry and their vehicle at the appointed place. Something is quite changed, though. Miss Pross is now permanently stone-deaf, caused by the crash of the pistol.

Commentary

Another of John Forster's objections to the *Tale* was the way in which Dickens disposed of the chief revolutionary agent in the plot—Madame Defarge. Replying to Forster's objections, Dickens wrote:

> I am not clear, and I never have been clear, respecting the canon of fiction which forbids the interposition of accident in such a case as Madame Defarge's death. Where the accident is inseparable from the passion and action of the character; where it is strictly consistent with the entire design, and arises out of some culminating proceeding on the part of the individual which the whole story has led up to; it seems to me to become, as it were, an act of divine justice. And when I use Miss Pross (though this is quite another question) to bring about such a catastrophe, I have the positive intention of making that half-comic intervention a part of the desperate woman's failure; and of opposing that mean death, instead of a desperate one in the streets which she wouldn't have minded, to the dignity of Carton's. Wrong or right, this was all design, and seemed to me to be in the fitness of things.

In this chapter, again, Dickens compares the powers of love and hate, this time in the persons of Miss Pross and Madame Defarge, respectively. He writes of "love, always so much stronger than hate."

QUESTION: What extra dimension does the scene between Miss Pross and Madame Defarge gain by the fact that the two women speak two different languages and, for the most part, do not understand what each other is saying?

CHAPTER 15

The Footsteps Die Out Forever

Summary

The tumbrils roll through the streets on that fatal day. The people are most curious about the man in the third cart—Sydney Carton, believed to be Charles Evrémonde, called Darnay—who looks at and speaks only with the young girl in the cart with him. John Barsad sees to his relief that Carton is going through with the sacrifice.

The Vengeance searches vainly for Madame Defarge to take her empty seat by the guillotine.

Continuing to comfort the little seamstress up to the very last moment, Sydney Carton follows her to his death. "They said of him, about the city that night, that it was the peacefullest man's face ever beheld there. Many added that he looked sublime and prophetic.''

The book ends with the prophetic and sublime thoughts that Sydney Carton would have uttered, if given a chance, as he went to his death. His final words are among the most famous in literature: ''It is a far, far better thing that I do, than I have ever done; it is a far, far better rest that I go to, than I have ever known.''

Commentary

Dickens issues a final warning to all oppressors of humanity: ''Crush humanity out of shape once more, under similar hammers, and it will twist itself into the same tortured forms. Sow the same seed of rapacious license and oppression over again, and it will surely yield the same fruit according to its kind.''

Carlyle's history provided several pieces of inspiration that Dickens seized upon for Carton's death. Carlyle includes Maton de la Varenne's account of his own narrow escape from death. In a pamphlet called ''Ma Resurrection'' Varenne recounts his terror and the wild events during the time he spent in prison. The resurrection theme, especially as it relates to Sydney Carton, proved useful to Dickens. Also in Carlyle's history is the story of Mme. Roland, a brave and noble lady who was sentenced to die. She requested a pen and paper ''to write the strange thoughts that were rising in her.'' Dickens clearly refers to her as the woman who ''had asked at the foot of the same scaffold, not long before, to be allowed to write down the thoughts that were inspiring her.'' This same woman had a friend who was timid about dying—hence, Dickens' little seamstress.

Generally, critics acclaim Sydney Carton's sacrifice as ''a deed of purification and redemption . . . and a triumphant assertion of the saving and creating power of love.'' They feel, however, that Carton's deed functions only on an individual level. It does not affect the continuing brutality and hatred of the Revolution. Dickens' final view of society, then (except for Carton's prophetic vision that is still ''long, long years to come''), is a pessimistic one. True to Dickens' probable intent, the *Tale* leaves us most vividly with scenes like the storming of the Bastille, the dancing of the Carmagnole, the sharpening of weapons at the grindstone, and the women knitting at the foot of the scaffold—scenes that are universally accepted as literary classics.

Character Sketches

As in his other novels, the people Dickens created in *A Tale of Two Cities* may be characterized as flat characters; that is, each person has a dominant characteristic obvious in his behavior on his first appearance and easily recognizable in his subsequent appearances. The flat character may be summed up in one sentence, but the manifestations of his dominant trait would require pages to enumerate. One advantage of the flat character is that he becomes fixed in the reader's mind and is easy to remember. After fixing the character in the mind of the reader, Dickens moves him through a multitude and variety of circumstances, surrounds him with a suggestion of suspense, gives him the key to unlock a mystery or the information to free one man and to send another to prison, puts him in the right place at the right time, and so on, with the result that he is always fresh and seemingly full of surprises. In *A Tale of Two Cities*, the reader enjoys a wide range of memorable persons, each good or bad in his individual way, each contributing to the great gallery of Dickens' famed characterizations.

Sydney Carton

No person in Dickens' gallery occupies a higher place than does Sydney Carton. Dickens stirs in the reader the same admiration he himself feels. From the beginning, Dickens impresses on the reader that Sydney Carton is, in essence, not what he seems to be. The reader recognizes his brilliant mind. He is first pictured slouching and indifferent at Darnay's trial, but he is quick to observe and act when he sees a way to save Darnay's life. He is a lonely man. "I care for no man on earth and no man on earth cares for me," he says soon after saving a man's life. He is an excessive drinker, the reader is told, but the reader never sees him when he is totally drunk, even as he leaves Stryver's rooms, where he exercises his powers of analysis in the preparation of Stryver's cases for presentation in court on the following day. After one such night, Dickens lets the reader glimpse into the mind and soul of Sydney. Sydney reveals a precise knowledge of himself and a sensitivity to the values that give life meaning—love, friendship, beauty and faith. He is unable to realize them in his own life. On the same night, Dickens gives the reader insight into Carton's youth as he and Stryver talk about their schooldays, when Sydney did the lessons of the other boys but not his own. Was he, even as a child, isolated by his own genius but seeking companionship?

Later, as a man still isolated and lonely, unable to find satisfaction in a society which values only material success, did he attempt to find refuge in drink? Two nights before he dies, Sydney walks the streets of Paris, his mind returning in a circle to his youth, to the early death of his mother, and to the death of his father when he was still a boy. This glimpse into Sydney's early life, so carefully recorded by

Dickens, suggests that the withdrawing of love from the life of the sensitive child holds the key to understanding the lack of incentive in school and the pattern of loneliness of his school and adult life.

It is not that Sydney is incapable of loving and inspiring love, but when love does touch him, it is a despairing love. Lucie cannot return his love, and his love for her cannot sustain him. Dickens introduces the affection of Lucie's two children to impress on the reader the innate worth of the man, for the two children are able to see beneath the surface as none of the adults, not even Lucie, can penetrate. At the end, his love and his faith give him the courage to expiate the waste of his life and to redeem himself. Sydney's final act of courage is not an inspired emotional response. It is, as are all acts of supreme courage, a deliberate, carefully reasoned act. To understand the deliberateness of his act, the reader must remember the promise Sydney made to Lucie before her marriage to Darnay, twelve years before the Reign of Terror, a promise carefully thought out before he came to see Lucie. Its fulfillment is even more carefully thought through. Sydney's sacrifice satisfies all of the criteria by which heroic acts today are judged to qualify for highest honors: it was beyond the call of duty; it was entirely voluntary; it was done with full advance knowledge of the risks involved; it was done after due deliberation.

Considering conditions in Paris in December, 1793, the reader may question what business brings Sydney Carton to Paris if not the affairs of Lucie. He arrives at Mr. Lorry's the day before Darnay's first appearance before the tribunal "to be useful," he says. The reader is not told how long he has been in Paris, but he is in full possession of all the facts of Darnay's case and knows the danger that awaits him. He has pried into Barsad's background and has planned how to blackmail him and to use him. His conversation with Mr. Lorry reveals his anticipation of death: his purchase of the potent drugs; the regression of his thoughts to the death of his parents and the words of faith spoken at his father's funeral, "I am the Resurrection and the Life . . ."; his comparison between his life and the swirling eddy of water suddenly finding its direction—all of these circumstances are evidence of the deliberate thoroughness of Carton's plan. To complete his preparations he visits the Defarges' wine-shop and then goes to Mr. Lorry to give him explicit instructions about leaving Paris. Assured that all their papers are in order, he gives Mr. Lorry his certificate, knowing that Darnay will fit the description on the certificate. After his last words of caution, Mr. Lorry says, "I will remember them. I hope to do my part faithfully." Sydney replies, "And I hope to do mine." He plans exactly how to handle Darnay in the death cell, carries out the last details, and goes to certain death. In death he achieves greatness, alone, with no one to give him encouragement and moral support. In death he achieves spiritual rebirth and, thus, Sydney's story of a waste life, his sufferings, his expiation, and his redemption, symbolizes Dickens' thematic interpretation of the French Revolution.

Dr. Manette

The importance which Dickens attached to Dr. Manette is suggested by the early titles he considered for the novel, *The Doctor of Beauvais, Long Ago*, and *Buried Alive*. Like Sydney Carton, Alexandre Manette possesses superior intelligence and is, by virtue of circumstances rather than by nature, a lonely man. Through the written account of his misfortunes, the reader knows that he was rising in his profession and was happily married when he was seized for having revealed the wrongs committed by a pair of nobles and was imprisoned and abandoned for eighteen years.

That he reported the wrongs of these nobles is evidence of his integrity and courage. Seemingly, the physical and emotional injuries of his imprisonment are obliterated by the loving care of Lucie. However, like Dickens himself, who always bore deep within him the psychological hurts of his childhood, Doctor Manette cannot always repress his psychological wounds or control his emotional responses when certain associations are set in motion. After his relapse, occasioned by Lucie's marriage to an Evrémonde, when Mr. Lorry advises the patient to curtail his activities, the doctor strongly advises against reduction of activity. He recommends that the patient (himself) pursue his studies, his experiments, and other healthful activities as a counterbalance to the strains of his life. This attitude seems to echo Dickens' own need of many and varied interests which he increased as the frustrations of his personal life became more distasteful and more imprisoning of his spirit. While crediting Lucie's unselfish love and care with setting free her father's mind and restoring his physical health, the reader should also recognize the active intelligence of Dr. Manette as a determining factor in his recovery. He fought, alone, in the Bastille to escape the frustrations of solitary confinement and, when first approached by Lucie and Mr. Lorry in the Defarges' attic, he fights painfully through the haze of his mind to reach them. During the fifteen months in Paris during the Reign of Terror, he fights unceasingly both to save Charles and to save hundreds among the oppressed and the oppressors. Dickens, likewise, plunged into frantic activity when he felt himself isolated from those whom he loved and had helped. The reader is not surprised to learn in Sydney's vision of the future that Dr. Manette continues, as an old man, to administer to his fellow man, a man of truly great moral courage.

Lucie Manette Darnay

Loving and beloved daughter, wife, mother, and friend, Lucie is almost too good to be true. At all times she reveals only those qualities that are universally admired and revered. In a tight-lipped attempt to conceal his feelings from Mr. Stryver, Sydney Carton calls her a "golden-haired doll." Indeed, her physical features are perfect in themselves, but Lucie's beauty goes far deeper than the mere physical. Her warmth and compassion restore life to Dr. Manette; they inspire Sydney Carton to commit the greatest act of his life; they give meaning to Miss Pross' life; and they make Lucie an ideal wife and mother. Although she tends to faint in overwhelming situations, she musters enough strength to stand outside La Force prison two hours every afternoon for a year and three months and she manages a courageous farewell when Charles is sentenced to die. Many people feel that Lucie represents the great love of Charles Dickens' own life at the time he was writing *A Tale of Two Cities*—the golden-haired actress named Ellen Ternan.

Charles Darnay

A perfect match for Lucie, Charles Evrémonde, called Darnay, embodies many of the ideal characteristics of physical, mental, and spiritual perfection that she does. Like Lucie, he always shows consideration for the feelings of others, especially in his relationships with Dr. Manette, Sydney Carton and, of course, Lucie. He stands in direct contrast to his evil uncle, the Marquis D'Evrémonde. Directly opposed to the "fear and slavery" philosophy that marks his uncle's handling of his tenants, Charles renounces his Evrémonde heritage and makes his own living in London as a tutor and translator. Hoping to redress the wrongs of his infamous family and to help an old servant in distress, Charles returns to Paris and thus motivates the action for the latter half of the novel.

With respect to plot, the novel centers around Charles Darnay. His acquittal at Old Bailey sets in motion the narrative that will eventually remove the Manette family from the comfort and security of London and directly involve them with the frightening characters and events in Revolutionary France.

Unlike Lucie, Charles does not generate life-giving qualities. He does not restore a father to life; he does not motivate Sydney Carton's resurrection (although he is a necessary part of it). His heroic mission to France in which he hoped to convince the French peasants to exercise restraint only ends in misery for himself and his family. Charles' intentions are always noble, however, and he always conducts himself as a poised and generous aristocrat.

The mirror-image of Sydney Carton, Darnay represents all the things that Carton could have been. But Charles Darnay could never have been Sydney Carton. He lacks the prophetic vision, the abject humility, and the desperate passion that characterize the greater man.

The Defarges

As a young boy, Ernest Defarge was a servant in the household of Dr. Manette in Paris. Having been treated with consideration, he retains a modicum of humanity. He is a leader of the Jacquerie, the underground movement plotting the revolution and directing it when it explodes. Revenge, craftiness, and cunning make him a leader in the years of plotting. Courage, violence, and fury give him powers of leadership in action when the citizens are called to arms to capture and burn the Bastille and to continue their mad pace for four more years.

Madame Defarge is a "frightfully grand woman," according to her husband. She shares with Carton the limelight of this drama of man's inhumanity to man. She is the antithesis of Carton, possessing not a single redeeming trait, feeling no remorse for wrong, feeling no need to atone, and finally going unredeemed to her death, in the very act of plotting new crimes, the deaths of the two Lucies. She is the revolutionary counterpart of the Marquis D'Evrémonde. Identified with him in the wrongs done to her family, she parallels his cruelty, singleness of purpose, indifference to the suffering of others, unshaken determination to pursue a way of oppression and sudden, violent death. Lest the reader waste sympathy on Madame Defarge when it is revealed that it is her family whom the Evrémondes had wronged, Dickens immediately reveals her in the act of plotting her last crimes and marching pitilessly toward the Manettes' lodgings. Dickens deliberately metes out to her an ignominious death in a quiet room at the hands of a woman whose name she does not know. She cannot have the glory of dying in battle for the Revolution. Her death is symbolic of the death of the soul through hate. Appropriately, her death deprives her of triumph at the very moment she expects to enjoy her goal of vengeance.

Mr. Jarvis Lorry

Mr. Lorry was, he insisted, first and foremost a man of business. At the beginning of the story, he was a man of sixty and he had been a man of business ever since he was a boy. He was an employee of Tellson's Bank and, for that reason, careful that his conduct should never be such as could do discredit to the house. Therefore, though he was a kindly man, he avoided speaking to Darnay before the latter had been acquitted of treason, and sheltering his dear friends, Lucie and Dr. Manette, in Tellson's Paris branch. His employer's confidence in him is shown when he was entrusted with the sole responsibility of making all arrangements for the departure from Paris of Lucie, her child, her enfeebled father, the servants, and Darnay.

In appearance Mr. Lorry was very neat and orderly, with his clothes planned to give evidence of a neatly turned leg, and a snowy wig. His face wore the carefully composed expression common to Tellson's bachelor clerks; but behind that expression lurked a glint of kindness. His relations with Miss Manette were those of thoughtful consideration, and his status with her father developed from that of a business advisor to that of friend. In Paris, when all seemed lost, the tears of this "good old man"—as Carton called him—were shed for the desolate young wife. Thanks to his friendship with the Manettes, Mr. Lorry no longer faced a lonely old age, but his place in a home.

Miss Pross

A strange-looking woman, brawny and "all red in colour," Miss Pross devotes herself to caring for the Manette family and, especially, her "Ladybird" (Lucie). Heartbroken over having been deserted by her brother, Solomon, she refuses to acknowledge the glaring fact that he "abandoned her in her poverty for evermore, with no touch of compunction." Her moment of glory comes near the end of the novel when "with the vigorous tenacity of love, always so much stronger than hate," she defeats Madame Defarge. Even the deafness which results from this encounter seems a small price to pay for the freedom of those she loves.

Jerry Cruncher

Primarily a comic figure, Jerry gradually develops into a highly sympathetic character. At first, he mystifies us with his "body-snatching" occupation, but eventually one of his nights in the cemetery pays off in the plot. As a "resurrection man" Jerry represents a comic and grotesque facet of the resurrection theme in the novel.

His tirades against the "flopping" (praying) of his "decent wife" and his colorful, uneducated dialect provide most of the humor in the novel.

Mrs. Cruncher ("Aggerawayter")

Jerry's long-suffering and "decent" wife, Mrs. Cruncher humbly submits to Jerry's verbal and even physical beatings. Because she disapproves of his "body-snatching," Jerry is convinced that she "flops" (prays) against him. By the end of the book he indicates much more sympathetic views towards her and her actions. "Aggerawayter," the name her husband often calls her, is doubtless a dialectal form of "aggravater," though the book does not explain this.

Solomon Pross (John Barsad)

First, he lost all of his sister's (Miss Pross') money and disappeared. Next, as a spy in England under the name "John Barsad," he testified against Charles Darnay. Then, working for the French king, he spied upon the Defarges and their wine-shop. And, finally, as a "sheep of the prisons," he worked for the French Revolutionists. As a mercenary opportunist, John Barsad is a loathsome creature. Only Sydney Carton's threats of exposure cause him to perform his one good act—allowing Charles Darnay to escape.

Roger Cly

Equal to Barsad in loathsomeness, a fellow spy who will work for whomever and whatever offers him gold, Roger Cly serves in a small way to implement the plot. He probably gets only what he deserves when the English mob, taunting and jeering, makes a mockery of his already mock funeral.

Stryver

Stryver is a boorish lawyer of no great ability, but with a driving ambition that enables him to "shoulder" his way upward in his profession and in his station in life. With considerable help from Sydney Carton, he successfully defends Charles Darnay in his London trial. Most of Stryver's success as a lawyer is due to Carton.

The Marquis D'Evrémonde

A cruel and tyrannical French aristocrat, the Marquis is the uncle of Charles Darnay. Although he is murdered early in the novel, the scene in which his carriage kills an innocent child in the suburb of Saint Antoine and the following scene in which he states his hatred towards his wretched tenants and his intentions to keep them in "fear and slavery" make a memorable impression. Dr. Manette's document, read much later in the novel, gives further evidence of his and his brother's (Charles' father) inhumanity.

Monseigneur

The Monseigneur represents all of the superficialities, inadequacies and selfishness of the French government against which the peasants rebel. He is first represented as a member of the French court, wallowing in luxury and totally oblivious to the needs of the people. Later, he is generalized to represent all such aristocrats whose homes and possessions were confiscated by the Revolutionists and who "took to [their] noble heels" and fled—mostly to England. Many of those who did not escape from France fell before the "patriots" guillotine.

Plot and Symbolism

Dickens did not come to the writing of *A Tale of Two Cities* until 1859, although from the time of the publication of Thomas Carlyle's *The French Revolution* in 1837, Dickens had had an enthusiastic admiration for his friend's book. The idea of the plot came to Dickens when he was playing in the melodrama *The Frozen Deep*, by Wilkie Collins, about a girl loved by two men, one of whom (this was the part Dickens played) sacrificed his life that the other man might live and marry the girl, who had shown a preference for the other man. After considering such titles as *One of These Days* and *Buried Alive* for his new novel, Dickens wrote to his friend—and later his biographer—John Forster, that he had found exactly the title he wanted, *A Tale of Two Cities*, and from that time on he wrote fast and was able to launch his new magazine, *All the Year Round*, in April, 1859, with the first instalment.

According to Forster, Dickens' first plan of the novel, as he had recorded it in his book of memoranda, was derived from his enjoyment of French drama. It was to be a story divided into two periods with a lapse of time between. Earle Davis explains how *A Tale of Two Cities* follows this plan. The comparatively short first book is similar to the prologue of the type of tragedy Dickens had in mind, and the second and third books, dealing with the main story, are comparable to the two long acts of French drama and are "balanced in length and action."

In the prologue of the first book, set in 1775, Dickens outlines the general conditions of unrest in England and France, predicts the outcome, establishes the atmosphere of discontent and mystery, introduces some of the main characters, suggests the main themes and symbols, and gives enough of the antecedent action to arouse the curiosity of the reader. In the first part of the second book, in 1780, Dickens brings in the remaining principal characters, starts the storyline, begins to enmesh the characters in personal and political complications, some of them obviously relating to the plot, some mystifying, and others so obscure that the reader is unaware of their importance at the time. Book II may seem dull in parts, but a rereading of the novel discloses how carefully Dickens created complications and laid the ground work for the violence and the crises that will erupt in the last book. The end of Book II skips to the year 1789, the storming of the Bastille, and gives a brief glimpse of the uprisings throughout France, and then skips again to 1792 in order to effect a transition to Book III.

Book III begins in 1792 and ends in December, 1793. The novel begins slowly, crammed with essential details, moves into the second book deliberately, picking up complications and momentum toward the end and, in the third book, rolls relentlessly from tragedy to tragedy, from violence to violence, and to a stunning climax. All of the unexplained relationships and complications are resolved, the mysteries and secrets are cleared up, punishments and rewards are meted out, and the curtain falls on a novel whose theatricality was deliberately and carefully contrived.

The French Revolution, by Carlyle, was the main source of Dickens' information for his novel with two settings, London and Paris. Adopting Carlyle's philosophy of history—for Dickens was neither scholar nor historian—Dickens created *A Tale of Two Cities* with its tightly structured plot, developed through a series of amazingly detailed and vivid pictures. For over a hundred years the scenes of this novel have so impressed themselves on the minds of its readers that for many this *is* the French Revolution: its causes rooted in generations of oppression and injustice; its course characterized by bloodshed, violence, vengeance, and death; and its outcome anticipating a regeneration, arising from the expiation of the evils of these times, the rebirth of a great nation, and the ushering in of the modern era.

Dickens once said that he had read Carlyle's history five hundred times. It is therefore natural that he came to see the Revolution as Carlyle saw it, a great human tragedy, for Dickens' own world was a world of people to whose sufferings he was always sensitive. Hence, his French Revolution was a tragedy of human beings, oppressors and oppressed alike, controlled by the events of history. Certainly, in detail after detail, Dickens acknowledged his debt to the historian. The attack on the Bastille, the murder of Foulon, the underground movement of the Jacobin Society, which Dickens calls the Jacquerie, the trials before the Revolutionary tribunals, the tumbrils, the guillotine, the slum section of Saint Antoine, the knitting women, even the finding of a letter in the archives of the Bastille—all are interpreted by Dickens as Carlyle saw them. From a book published in Amsterdam, Mercier's *Tableaux de Paris*, Dickens borrowed an atrocity or two. It is also interesting that the idea of Dr. Manette's turning to making shoes as an escape from his mental torment may have come from a hobby pursued by Louis XVI. The king worked at locksmithing to escape from the rigors of ruling. The final vision of Sydney Carton was inspired by Carlyle's account of the request of Madame Roland, who asked as she was about to ascend the steps to the guillotine that she be permitted to write down her thoughts. Nor should it be forgotten that Dickens had accumulated much information in France in the course of his extended sojourns there in the 1840's. Many people who had lived through the Revolution were still alive. Memories of the Revolution were fresh in the minds of children and grandchildren of those who had lived through the period and life in Paris and in the provinces had changed little from its customary course in the late eighteenth century.

Railroads had not come into being; Dickens himself travelled in the same way as Mr. Lorry and the Manettes did.

Dickens says at the end of the novel's opening chapter: "Thus did the year one thousand seven hundred and seventy-five conduct their Greatnesses, and myriads of small creatures—the creatures of this chronicle among the rest—along the roads that lay before them." Dickens leaves no doubt that he intends to show that the lives of all of the people of his story are connected and controlled by fate, that the destinies of the great will merge with the destinies of the small, and that people remote from one another in place and in position will follow roads that will converge in Paris in the year 1793.

Dualism, always a significant characteristic of Dickens' craft, is clearly proclaimed in the title *A Tale of Two Cities*. How to balance and connect the two cities is a problem Dickens solved by a number of devices—symbols, characters, fate, and plot structure. The first and most obvious symbol is the symbol of the road, the London-Calais road and the Calais-Paris road. In addition to the road, which is to be taken both literally and symbolically, he introduces other symbols and connects the two cities through his characters whose lives influence each other in a series of fateful coincidences of circumstances and events. He fuses all of these elements into a harmonious whole to develop his themes of wrong, expiation and regeneration, of hatred and revenge, and of love and sacrifice.

When the narrative begins in Chapter 2, three people, Mr. Lorry, Miss Pross, and Lucie Manette, and a fourth, later to be presumed to be Charles Darnay, travel the Dover road on their way from London towards Paris in November, 1775. A few days later, all return by the same road, accompanied by another principal character, Dr. Manette. Without their knowing it or willing it, this trip changes the course of life of every person in the story. Throughout the novel, the road between London and Paris connects the creatures of the story by travel and by communication. The dangers of the Dover road and the mists along the way foreshadow the dangers and the mists that will engulf the characters on the road of life. Finally, this road provides the escape route the same characters will take out of the dangers of Paris to the safety of London in December, 1793.

Plot and Fate

Dickens uses fate to create a number of character links between the two cities. Most significant in the fate of the main characters is the physical resemblance between the French-speaking Englishman, Sydney Carton, and the English-speaking Frenchman, Charles Darnay. This resemblance enables Carton to twice save the life of Darnay, first in a London courtroom and second in a Paris prison. Both love the same girl, born in Paris of a French father and an English mother, and living in London.

It was Mr. Lorry's fate that he should spend his early years in Tellson's Paris bank, where he conducted the affairs of the Manettes, that he should be assigned to take Lucie to London when she was only two years old, and that he should re-enter her life when charged with taking her to Paris to rescue her father. Because of his early experience in Paris, Mr. Lorry is given the heavy responsibility of directing Tellson's in Paris during the Reign of Terror, and this assignment is a coincidence that enables him to help the Manettes in Paris and finally to escape. In London, Tellson's becomes the meeting place of the French émigrés and the center of information about events in Paris. Even Jerry Cruncher, Mr. Lorry's odd-job man at Tellson's both in London and in Paris, becomes a connecting link when, in Paris, he furnishes incriminating evidence against John Barsad which he had collected in London.

In the last scene, fate brings together an improbable pair, the brilliant English lawyer and the illiterate French seamstress. Dr. Manette is, of course, the basic link tying together the characters, the cities, and the theme. It was his fate as a doctor in Paris to incur the hostility of the powerful St. Evrémonde brothers, to be imprisoned by them through a lettre de cachet, and to be released eighteen years later in the care of his daughter, Lucie. In London, his daughter is fated to fall in love with, and to marry, the son of an Evrémonde who will one day be sentenced to pay for the wrong done to his father-in-law. Events return them all to Paris, where the doctor tries to use his influence as a former Bastille prisoner to save his son-in-law. Dr. Manette, therefore, is a link among the characters and a link between the oppressions of the past and the vegeance of the Revolution. In his suffering, his living death, and his restoration to life, Dr. Manette is an echo of Dickens' thematic interpretation of the Revolution.

Blood Imagery

Besides the pervading symbol of the road, the first scene in Paris introduces the symbol of blood when Gaspard, dipping his fingers in the muddied wine in the Saint Antoine Street, scrawls "BLOOD" on the wall of a shop. Much blood is to be spilled between the time when the red wine stains the ground and the blood of the victims of the Revolution stains the ground at the site of the guillotine. The red of the blood is transferred with ominous connotations to other situations, to the red sunset over the château of the Evrémondes, to the fire consuming the château, to the red caps worn by the citizen patriots, to the gory heads on pikes and to the tumbrils carrying the day's wine to the guillotine. The way in which Dickens continued to widen and extend the connotation of blood and red illustrates the way symbols are used in literature. A symbol does not have one meaning. It continually extends its meanings, picks up additional meanings, and often takes on opposing meanings, all the time enriching and giving depth to the context.

As an example consider the scene in which the sunset illuminates the travelling carriage of the Marquis as he nears home. Literally, it means the end of a day. Symbolically, it recalls the shedding of the run-over child's blood. It suffuses the face of the Marquis with a red color; his blood is to be spilled that night. The sun is setting on the life of the Marquis. Later, his château will be set afire, reddening the sky. It signals the literal destruction of the château and of all the family. It symbolizes similar uprisings and similar destruction throughout France. At first, red evokes sympathy for the oppressed people of France. Later, it evokes sympathy for the victims of the Revolution. Every time the symbol of red, of fire, and of blood recurs in the novel, the symbol extends its meaning, both literally and connotatively, and it contributes unity to all of the situations in which it is used.

Footsteps

Early in Book II, Dickens brings in the echoing footsteps at the corner of Soho Square as a symbol to link the quiet life there with the mad and dangerous footsteps that will surround the Manettes in Paris. Both sets of footsteps are outside the Manette household. The Manettes can neither control nor escape them. Darnay is responsible for bringing the footsteps of Paris into the lives of his family; yet he acts not of his own volition, for he is lured to the "Loadstone Rock." The consequences are events which draw him and his family involuntarily to Paris. Only Sydney Carton accepts the footsteps and the consequences voluntarily.

Love and Hate

Home and prison are used by Dickens to symbolize love and hate. But Dickens saw that a clear separation of the two would be an oversimplification. Hence, he shows love penetrating into the prison and hate penetrating into the home. Dr. Manette is an illustration of the hate in men's souls that can send to prison an innocent man. Dr. Manette, after ten years of isolation, becomes contaminated by hate in the atmosphere of the physical prison and in the emotional and psychological prison of his own spirit. In that hate he composes a document that will almost wreck the lives of those he loves best. His daughter's love restores him, but not completely.

The loving atmosphere of the Manette household spiritually nourishes everyone who is welcomed there—the doctor, Lucie, Mr. Lorry, Miss Pross, Charles Darnay, and Sydney Carton. The same love is transported to Paris. But into that home, hate penetrates in the person of Madame Defarge, and in that home takes place the love-hate struggle between Madame Defarge and Miss Pross, symbolizing the triumph of love over hate. Madame Defarge, untouched by love, cannot escape from her personal prison of hate. The prisons of Paris are cells of hate into which love penetrates. When he is transferred to the Conciergerie, Sydney Carton gains entrance to his cell, motivated by the greatest love of which man is capable. During the fifteen months Charles is in prison, Dr. Manette seeks to have him freed, meanwhile leading a busy life, ministering out of love for suffering humanity to the ills of both the prisoners and their oppressors. Dickens' personal experiences with prisons had been of a dual nature. He had seen debtors helping each other in Marshalsea prison and he had observed criminality of the lowest order in the many prisons he had visited. Dickens seemed to have an obsessive interest in prisons, for wherever he travelled, in the United States, France, Italy and in his own country, he made it a practice to visit prisons. Dickens uses prisons in a symbolic way to represent the miseries that human beings are subject to.

Water

Another symbol that became almost obsessive with Dickens was the river as a symbol of life. The symbol does not remain constant; it might be a river, or it might be a fountain, an eddy, a wave, or the sea. It might cleanse, or it might poison; it could save, or it could kill. Dickens states in Chapter 7 of the second book, after the killing of the child by the carriage of the Marquis: "The water of the fountain ran, the swift river ran, the day ran into evening, so much life in the city ran into death according to rule . . . all things ran their course." This passage suggests an elaborate extension of the symbol throughout the novel. In the village of the Marquis, the fountain was the center of life. The night that death came to the Marquis, "the fountain in the village flowed unseen and unheard, and the fountain at the château dropped unseen and unheard, both melting away, like the minutes that were falling from the spring of Time," and when day dawned, "the water of the château fountain seemed to run to blood . . ."

When Gaspard is hanged for killing the Marquis, his body is suspended over the fountain to deny the villagers the life-giving waters of the fountain. Dickens likens the mob storming the Bastille to a "sea of black and threatening waters," "the remorseless sea." The uprisings occurring in the provinces are described in a chapter entitled, "The Sea Still Rises." After Sydney has determined upon his course, he walks along the Seine, ". . . watching the eddy that turned and turned purposelessly, until the stream absorbed it, and carried it on to the sea—'Like me!'" In the chapter entitled "Fifty-two" Dickens equates time and the flowing waters. The fifty-two victims, compared to the weeks of the year, are "to roll that afternoon on the life-tide of the city to the boundless everlasting sea." Dickens says as Sydney is guillotined, "The murmuring of many voices, the upturning of many faces, the pressing on of many footsteps in the outskirts of the crowd, so that it swells forward in a mass, like one great heave of water, all flashes away.''

Pictures

When Dickens decided that the overall structure of the novel would follow the structure of French drama, he also decided to develop the plot as a series of pictures. He said in a letter: ''But I set myself the little task of making a *picturesque* story, rising in every chapter, with characters true to nature, but whom the story should express more than they should express themselves by dialogue.'' Most of the chapters are self-contained pictures. Each picture has its center of interest, all details contributing to that focus and creating a single mood or atmosphere appropriate to the central theme, the overall purpose being to evoke a specific emotional response in the reader. In some chapters there is a break, with two contrasting or balancing pictures. Some chapters are vast canvases of humanity gone mad; some are small tableaux of human beings, gentle and loving. Always, Dickens makes the reader see, hear, and feel. In these pictures, Dickens makes the reader see not an anonymous crowd, but identifiable individuals having a definite relation to the theme of the picture and to the theme of the novel. In the wine-cask scene there is pathos in the people's attempts at gaiety and celebration in the midst of grinding poverty. This scene is reenacted years later, the gaiety magnified to frightening dimensions in the picture of Carmagnole. Horror-struck, the reader sees five hundred demons dancing in wild abandon, hears their shouts, feels the savage rhythm of *La Marseillaise*—all in celebration of the last batch of victims of the guillotine. In the time between these two scenes are the spectacles of the storming and burning of the Bastille, the burning of the château seen from the perspective of the gratified villagers, and the awful people at their awful work at the grindstone. Each chapter in the novel makes its particular contribution to the picturing of the plot and the characters being manipulated by the plot.

The instrument which dominates Book III is pictured for the first time in the final scene. High on a platform, its uprights and blade outlined against the sky, the guillotine awaits fifty-two victims. The tumbrils line up to discharge their cargo and the rows of chairs are filled with knitting women (only one is empty). Dickens halts the action to let the reader see into the mind of Sydney Carton. ''I am the Resurrection and the Life . . . he that believeth in me shall never die.'' The reader sees a man expiating his wasted life and coming to a spiritual rebirth. In Carton's vision of the future, Dickens identifies Carton with the theme of his tale, a nation expiating the evils of generations and coming slowly to regeneration and rebirth. A brilliant novel, *A Tale of Two Cities* rises steadily in power and drama and ends on a note of exaltation.

Theme

From the beginning of the narrative with Mr. Lorry's message "Recalled to Life," to the end with Sydney Carton's "I am the Resurrection and the Life . . ." Dickens repeatedly insists on the theme of regeneration. In his own time, in his own country, and in his travels, Dickens observed oppresion. He saw class pitted against class, humanity crushed by humanity. He saw the need for the individual crusader and reformer. For him, the hope for the future came to mean regeneration, individual regeneration making possible the regeneration of society. In the final chapter of *A Tale of Two Cities,* Dickens says:

> Crush humanity out of shape once more, under similar hammers, and it will twist itself into the same tortured forms. Sow the same seed of rapacious license and oppression over again, and it will surely yield the same fruit according to its kind.
>
> Six tumbrils roll along the streets. Change these back again to what they were, powerful enchanter, Time, and they shall be seen to be the carriages of absolute monarchs, equipages of feudal nobles, the toilettes of flaming Jezebels, the churches that are not my father's house but dens of thieves, the huts of millions of starving peasants! No; the great magician who majestically works out the appointed order of the Creator never reverses his transformation.

This passage is not an interruption of the narrative taking Carton to the guillotine but an integral part of Dickens' theme: the only remedy for moral and social disorder is moral regeneration of the individual. Justice and right are the proper concern of the individual. Sydney Carton's courage and sacrifice are not an isolated dramatic instance of sacrifice but a symbol of individual courage and sacrifice throughout history. Society depends upon the individual. The individual who has the moral courage—and if need be, the physical courage—to break the fetters of his self-prison is the hope of the world. That is what *A Tale of Two Cities* is all about; this is what makes it not just a tale of two cities during the French Revolution, but a tale of all places and all times. This is what makes the French Revolution a revolution of people everywhere breaking the bonds of oppression and of all that imprisons the human spirit. The theme of regeneration of the individual gives the book as much pertinence today as it had in Dickens' time, perhaps more. It is Dickens' answer to the question "Am I my brother's keeper?"

In terms of the plot, this theme of regeneration is embodied as a series of rescues; the rescue being the most physical and dramatic method of saving a man. There is no necessary connection between these two, since a man can rescue or be rescued and still be spiritually unredeemed. But Dickens makes the connection plausible and even essential in this novel. If a man is not worth loving, one infers, who would take the trouble to rescue him?

Dickens takes pains to draw a hierarchy of values between the minimal rescue and the rescue involving a total self-sacrifice. On the lowest level, there is Sydney Carton's rescue of Charles Darnay during his English trial. Carton himself refers to this as merely a piece of legal claptrap. It requires no self-sacrifice and no affection for the person rescued. But, at the highest level, there is Carton's final rescue of Darnay and his family. This requires a complete self-sacrifice that comes from a total affection.

Between these two extremes we find other rescues that fill in the spectrum. There is Mr. Lorry's trip to Paris in Book I, where he delivers Dr. Manette from his French garret. Although this is undertaken as business for Tellson's, it rises above Carton's legal rescue because Mr. Lorry shows a personal concern for Dr. Manette and Lucie. Then, there is Charles Darnay's trip to France to save Gabelle, who is released from jail only because Darnay has been imprisoned. This rescue is based on family honor, but it is clouded by well-meaning vanity and an ignorance of the consequences on Darnay's part. Finally, there are Dr. Manette's two rescues of Darnay, the first from mob slaughter and the second at his trial (which proves ineffective). Manette works tirelessly for a year and three months in his effort to save Darnay, and he does it to repay his daughter. It is a heroic attempt, but it lacks the transcendent quality of Carton's final rescue.

There are other means of saving people than rescuing them from death, and Dickens deals with these as well. Dr. Manette is saved from insanity and poor health through his daughter's care and affection. Mr. Lorry is saved from a sterile business life through his friendship with the Manettes. Miss Pross is saved from her natural isolation through her devotion to Lucie. Sydney Carton is saved from his reckless, wasted life because of his love for Lucie. At the lowest level of the reborn there is Jerry Cruncher, whose salvation consists of repenting his wrongdoing, vowing not to return to it, and harboring an unselfish wish that the Darnays may escape from France. But affection as an agent of rebirth is a mutual thing, and these people are, in a sense, both the rescued and the rescuers.

In interweaving the rescued and the rescuers, Dickens shows how much people need each other to survive. Dickens' good characters are mutually dependent. In a world with so much evil they have to be. What would Dr. Manette have if his son-in-law were executed and his daughter died of grief? What would Mr. Lorry or Miss Pross have if their friends were wiped out? What would Sydney Carton have if Lucie and her family died when he could have saved them?

At the center of this pattern is Lucie, the most vulnerable person in the novel. Her life explicitly depends on the lives of her loved ones. Unable to rescue anyone directly, her power derives from her concern and love for others, which in turn gives courage to them. She is the passive, radiating center about whom the other redeemed people orbit.

All of this redemption takes place against a background of damnation that grows more intense as the novel progresses. The accelerating action calls forth more extreme efforts at salvation. There are many characters who are wholly damned. These are types who are completely self-involved, like Stryver and the French aristocrats, or who do mischief for self-advancement, like Barsad and Cly, or who take delight in exterminating those who differ with them, like the mobs or Madame Defarge and her associates. These people have forgotten the original purpose of the Revolution: they enjoy the spectacle of murder for its own sake. This is the ultimate degradation of humanity in Dickens' view, a degradation that needs a heroic self-sacrifice to redeem what is worth saving.

Style

Dickens' style is everything Dickens touches and how he touches it. It is his special manner of treating his characters, plots, and descriptions, his special forms of expression, his techniques of creating audio-visual and emotional situations. True, he writes sentences that are too long and too detailed; he uses circumlocution instead of simple, forthright statement. He is sometimes overly sentimental. In *A Tale of Two Cities,* the first interview between Lucie and her father is scarcely natural, and the farewell scene between Charles and Lucie in the Paris tribunal is a situation more likely to leave a couple bereft of words. In Dickens, characters prove their love more convincingly by their actions than by their words. But his clear purpose was to make his readers see, feel, and hear, and he labored to perfect a style that would accomplish his purpose. He so succeeded in fusing the elements of his style that it is only by analysis that the reader becomes aware of the discrete elements of his style.

First, Dickens worked to achieve precision of diction. His words and phrases must not only denote exact literal meaning, but they must also be capable of extended meanings and interpretations. Consider the famous sentence: "It was the best of times, it was the worst of times . . ." in which each pair of alternates relates precisely to the year 1775 and can be extended to relate to every period in history. Or observe how the following passages make the reader imagine with his senses and carry him backward or forward in time in the larger context and meaning of the novel: "a steaming mist in all the hollows," "a people who had undergone a terrible grinding and regrinding in the mill," "the baffled blueflies were dispersing in search of other carrion," "muskets in a most explosive state of readiness," "the ghost of beauty, the ghost of stateliness, the ghost of elegance," "the whole jury, as a jury of dogs, empanelled to try the deer," "Six tumbrils carry the day's wine to the guillotine." Dickens perfection of metaphoric language enabled him to fuse situation, atmosphere, and tone with language that communicated his meaning precisely.

In characterization, Dickens imitated the methods of the eighteenth and early nineteenth-century novelists, notably Smollett and Sir Walter Scott, but he superimposed his own style, and that made all the difference. Caricature, which became the trademark of Dickens' early works and which his readers came to expect, is used sparingly in *A Tale of Two Cities.* The de-emphasis on this aspect of Dickens' style disturbed his readers, but the serious tone of Dickens' later works precludes comic caricature. The wildness and eccentricities of Miss Pross are a foil for Lucie Manette's gentleness and ladylike comportment. Jerry Cruncher's hoarse voice, close-set eyes, spiked hair and ridiculous clothes serve as a comic contrast to the ultra-conservative Mr. Lorry, and his literal employment of the term "Resurrection-man" is a light but significant rendering of the resurrection theme. Jerry illustrates another stylistic device that Dickens borrowed, the tag. Jerry repeatedly refers to himself with the tag "an honest tradesman." He identifies his wife by the tags "Aggerawayter" and "floppin'." Mr. Lorry carries the tag "a man of business." Tags are very useful to the reader. They permit him to make immediate identification with a character when that character reappears. When Dickens refers to the Lion, the Jackal, the man of delicacy, or The Vengeance, the reader calls forth a distinct mental image, whether Dickens is using the term literally or satirically.

A Tale of Two Cities is not typical of Dickens in that there is a single plot instead of his usual multi-plot technique. But other elements of his style are present: the telling of the story by means of exciting scenes with conflicting forces; good triumphing over evil; a host of coincidences to assist fate in carrying characters to their destiny; and the use of theatrical and melodramatic effects to stir the emotions of the reader, preferably to tears. There are stage effects in the incredible sumptuousness of Monseigneur's reception, pictured as a fancy dress ball, at which every guest was disfigured by "the leprosy of unreality." Dickens' picturing of the storming of the Bastille is punctuated by staccato notes to heighten the emotion: "Headlong mad and dangerous footsteps . . . deep ditches, double drawbridges, massive stone walls . . . two fierce hours . . . deep ditch, single drawbridge, massive stone walls . . . Work, comrades all, work! . . . The prisoners! . . . The Records! . . . The secret cells! . . . ," "The remorseless sea of turbulently swaying shapes, voices of vengeance, and faces hardened in the furnaces of suffering until the touch of pity could make no mark on them." The melodrama in the trials of Darnay before the revolutionary tribunal is supplied by the appearance of the judges, looking like felons, and the turbulent audience, composed of the lowest, cruelest, and worst populace of the city of Paris, noisily approving and disapproving, cheering and shedding tears after his acquittal, and roaring their revengeful approval as each juryman voted for Charles' death after the reading of Dr. Manette's letter.

There is exciting melodrama in the scene in which the Evrémonde château burns. Against the gloom of the night, the flames rise forty feet high; the village bell rings impatiently while two hundred villagers stand impassive before appeals for help; masses of stone and timber fall crashing; and when the destruction is complete, the village bell rings for joy. Madame Defarge's hopes have begun to be realized. Madame Defarge, an illiterate peasant woman, is given eloquent lines to describe the whirlwind the Jacquerie is preparing and to reveal the secret of her revenge: ". . . I was brought up among the fishermen of the seashore, and that peasant family so injured by the two Evrémonde brothers, as that Bastille paper describes, is my family. Defarge, that sister of the mortally wounded boy upon the ground was my sister, that husband was my sister's husband, that unborn child was their child, that brother was my brother, that father was my father, those dead are my dead, and that summons to answer for those things descends to me!'' These are lines out of Victorian melodrama. In fact, Dickens, in making the melodramatic an integral element of his style, was reflecting the artistic tastes of his times. The readings Dickens gave of his own works were played before packed houses and were applauded tumultuously because they were highly emotionalized versions of his writings. But not all the scenes are melodrama. In the death scene, when Sydney Carton ascends the steps to the guillotine, there is tragic drama.

Many of the melodramatic scenes are horror scenes. Dickens' use of horror is another borrowing from earlier novelists, notably Sir Walter Scott, for whom Dickens had sincere admiration. The melodramatic horror scenes are fused with another element of Dickens' style, his use of contrasts and/or alternating scenes. The killing of Gaspard's child in the streets of Saint Antoine by the carriage of the Marquis follows the fancy dress ball; the killing of the Marquis by the revengeful Jacques contrasts with the compassion expressed by Charles for the peasants oppressed by his family; the storming of the Bastille follows a peaceful scene in the gardens of the Manette household in Soho; the firing of the château eventually brings Charles Darnay from the peace of his London home to the chaos of Paris; the brutality of the demons sharpening their blood-stained weapons contrasts with the peace within Mr. Lorry's lodgings and the love which motivates Mr. Lorry's visitors; the frenzied patriots that participated most vigorously in the hanging of Foulon became gentle parents that evening as they played with their children after the day's work was over.

The method by which Dickens chose to tell his story, that is, by a series of descriptive scenes, required him to practise all the techniques of his craft in order to produce a unified work of art. Of all the elements of his style which went into creating unity of impression throughout *A Tale of Two Cities*, none is more skilful than Dickens' manipulation of his symbols. Introduced early and repeated throughout the novel, all serve to give unity and significance to the story. The student today who learns to identify the symbols and to follow them through their widening connotations comes to a deeper understanding of the novel and to an appreciation of Dickens that readers of his own time failed to enjoy. It is through his metaphoric and symbolic language that Dickens makes *A Tale of Two Cities* not only a tale of London and Paris during a period of change and upheaval but a tale with a larger context, the story of man rising up against oppression everywhere and struggling for human dignity and freedom.

Literary Elements

Names

Dickens often uses a name to suggest the quality of a character, a device borrowed from Fielding and Smollett. In this novel, *Stryver* is obvious. *Charles Darnay* bears the author's initials. *Mr. Lorry* suggests his function as a means of conveyance. *Dr. Manette* is "man" with a diminutive. *Evrémonde* hints at Everyman or Everyworld. *Gabelle,* the tax-collector, bears the name of the hated tax on salt. The effect of this technique is to make the characters appear more as types, or allegorical figures, than they necessarily are.

Animal Images

These are used symbolically to convey the essence of a person or a group, to suggest status, or to point to bestiality. Darnay's uncle is seen as tigerish. A crowd of poor people are viewed as rats. The spectators at Darnay's English trial are presented as blue-flies in search of carrion. Jerry Cruncher is referred to as an English bulldog (which reminds us, incidentally, that he digs up buried bones). When we first meet Mr. Lorry, getting out of the coach at Dover, he is like a dog, not in a negative sense but referring to his fidelity. And, of course, Carton's relation to Stryver is that of a jackal to a lion.

Humor

This element is almost exclusively confined to the passages involving Jerry Cruncher and Miss Pross. It is of a grim, grotesque, or absurd nature, and appears as relief after tense situations. Miss Pross supplies the first example on the occasion of Lucie's fainting after hearing the banker's story of her father, when she vows that Providence never intended her to cross salt water by casting her lot on an island. She shows it again in her exchange of remarks with her brother, Jerry Cruncher, and Mme Defarge in her shopping experiences in Paris. Cruncher's humor is greatest before and after his work in robbing graves. Stryver's discomfort in his attempt to confer the honor of his hand on Lucie is mildly humorous, as is also Mr. Lorry's resort to a "business" excuse when he found himself in a difficulty.

Pathos

Our sympathies are aroused frequently: the first meeting of Lucie and her father; Carton's confession of his love and resignation to Lucie; Dr. Manette's valiant struggle for recovery; Lucie's faithful attendance beneath Darnay's cell window; Carton's sacrifice, and his brave words of encouragement to the little seamstress.

Melodrama

Dickens drew much inspiration from the English stage, inheriting all of its melodramatic machinery. Lost inheritances, disguises, blood curses, secret sins, innocent victims—these are stage conventions from time immemorial. But Dickens' imagination was naturally impelled toward the startling, the hidden, the dramatic. Being an extrovert, he needed to embody his mental impulses in action. He is at his best (and often at his worst) in the theatrical confrontation of his characters. His scenes follow one another swiftly with a minimal amount of connecting material. His characters are usually simple but are endowed with vividness, energy, and strong emotions. Moreover, they are surrounded by props that tend to take on a life of their own, like Madame Defarge's knitted "shrouds." Everything appears to be alive and full of dramatic potential.

Coincidence

Modern readers find Dickens' use of coincidence as artificial and stylized as the tradition of melodrama from which it derived. In this novel, Dickens saves up most of his coincidences until Chapter 10 of Book III, in Dr. Manette's manuscript, where they begin to test one's credulity. Much that was mysterious is explained, and we tend to accept this as we would the logic of a fairy tale. Nevertheless, in showing so directly the connections between some major characters, Dickens draws attention to a serious idea that underlies all of his fiction: that all men are brothers for better or worse, that people are frequently related to one another in secret ways, and that every crime against human brotherhood must be paid for in kind.

Personification

This process is allied to symbolism—it endows inanimate objects and abstract ideas with life. The destruction of Dr. Manette's cobbling equipment seems to Mr. Lorry and Miss Pross to be like a murder, as if the equipment were semi-human. The guillotine is canonized as a saint. The Marquis D'Evrémonde personifies abstract Privilege, just as Madame Defarge personifies abstract Revenge. Much of this process takes place in the French sections of the novel, where Dickens is technically forced to use these symbols to portray the panorama of oppression and revolution.

Suspense

Suspense is possibly the lowest, and yet the most basic, element of the plot. Dickens achieves it, first of all, by throwing his virtuous characters into difficulties and then staging rescues for them. The hero, Darnay, repeatedly gets himself into difficulties from which he has to be rescued. Another device that Dickens employs is to insert mysterious occurrences, like Barsad's appearances or Cruncher's "honest trade," and to solve them in the course of events.

A Tale of Two Cities Reconsidered

A Tale of Two Cities ends fairly cheerfully with its hero getting killed; Dickens's previous novel, *Little Dorrit,* ends in deep gloom with its hero getting married. Violence offers Dickens a partial release from the sense of frustration and despondency which crept over him during the eighteen-fifties; the shadow of the Marshalsea lifts a little with the storming of the Bastille, and everyone remembers *A Tale of Two Cities* above all for the intoxication of its crowd-scenes. In fact they take up less space than one supposes in retrospect, and for the most part the atmosphere is every bit as stifling as that of *Little Dorrit*. Dickens originally thought of calling the book *Buried Alive*, and at its heart lie images of death and, much less certainly, of resurrection: themes which foreshadow *Our Mutual Friend*.

The story opens with the feeblest of resurrections, the recall to life of Doctor Manette. His daughter is afraid that she is going to meet his ghost, a fear that is almost justified when she actually sees his spectral face and hears his voice, so faint and lacking in life and resonance that it is 'like the last feeble echo of a sound made long and long ago . . . like a voice underground'. (Bk. I, Ch. 6.) The whole novel is thronged with ghosts; from the mist moving forlornly up the Dover Road 'like an evil spirit seeking rest and finding none' to the gunsmoke which as it clears suggests Madame Defarge's soul leaving her body, there are scores of references to spectres, phantoms, and apparitions. The penniless émigrés haunt Tellson's like familiar spirits; Lorry sees the likeness of the Lucie whom he once knew pass like a breath across the pier-glass behind her; the fountains of the château show ghostly in the dawn—but it would be tedious to compile a catalogue.

Such ghostliness suggests, first of all, a sense of unreality, of the death in life to which men are reduced by imprisonment, psychological or actual. To Darnay, the prisoners in La Force, going through the motions of elegance and pride in the midst of squalor, are ghosts all, 'waiting their dismissal from the desolate shore', and the scene simply 'the crowning unreality of his long unreal ride'. (Bk. III, Ch. 1.) But ghosts are also the creatures of false or, at any rate, imperfect resurrection: the grave gives up its dead reluctantly, and the prisoner who has been released is still far from being a free man. The inmates of the Bastille, suddenly given their liberty by 'the storm that had burst their tomb', are anything but overjoyed: 'all scared, all lost, all wondering and amazed, as if the Last Day were come, and those who rejoiced around them were all lost spirits'. (Bk. II, Ch. 21.) Even the phlegmatic Darnay, after his Old Bailey acquittal, 'scarcely seems to belong to this world again'. As for Doctor Manette, he has been as

*Editor's title. By John Gross. From "A Tale of Two Cities," in Dickens and the Twentieth Century, edited by John Gross and Gabriel Pearson. Copyright ©1962 by Routledge & Kegan Paul Ltd. Reprinted by permission.

deeply scarred by his prison experience as William Dorrit. Lucie's love is not enough in itself to stop him from retreating into his shoe-making, and it takes a symbolic act of violence to complete the cure; he is fully restored to himself only after Mr. Lorry has hacked to pieces his cobbler's bench, 'while Miss Pross held the candle as if she were assisting at a murder'. (Book II, Ch. 19.) But by this time the centre of interest in the book has shifted unmistakably to Sydney Carton.

The prison and the grave are linked in Dickens's mind with the idea that 'every human creature is constituted to be that profound secret and mystery to every other'. We live in essential isolation; in each heart there is, 'in some of its imaginings, a secret to the heart nearest it. Something of the awfulness, even of death itself, is referable to this . . . In any of the burial-places of this city through which I pass, is there a sleeper more inscrutable than its busy inhabitants are, in their innermost personality, to me, or than I am to them?' (Bk I, Ch. 3.) On his journey to greet the newly released Manette, Mr. Lorry feels as if he is going to unearth a secret as well as dig up a dead man; in his dream the grave is confused with the underground strong-rooms at Tellson's, and he fancies himself digging 'now with a spade, now with a great key, now with his hands'. In his hotel room, the two tall candles are reflected on every leaf of the heavy dark tables, 'as if *they* were buried in deep graves of dark mahogany, and no light to speak of could be expected of them until they were dug out'. (Bk. I, Ch. 4.)

This oppressive sense of mystery generates suspicion and fear. 'All secret men are soon terrified', Dickens tells us in connection with Bar-sad, the police spy; but we are in a world where everyone is a secret man, a world of whispers and echoes. On the Dover Mail 'the guard suspected the passengers, the passengers suspected one another and the guard, they all suspected everybody else'; when Darnay returns to France, 'the universal watchfulness so encompassed him, that if he had been taken in a net, or were being forwarded to his destination in a cage, he could not have felt his freedom more completely gone'. (Bk. III, Ch. 1.) Even in the haven established for Doctor Manette near Soho Square there is foreboding in the air, in the echoes which Lucie makes out to be 'the echoes of all the footsteps that are coming by and by into our lives'. An accurate enough premonition of the noise of feet and voices pouring into the Paris courtyard which first draws her attention to the bloodstained grindstone, or of the troubled movement and shouting round a street-corner which herald the Carmagnole. Carton's last impression, too, is to be of 'the pressing on of many footsteps' on the outskirts of the crowd round the guillotine. Footsteps suggest other people, and in *A Tale of Two Cities* other people are primarily a threat and a source of danger. This little group around Doctor Manette is as self-contained as any in Dickens, but it enjoys only a precarious safety; the emblematic golden arm on the wall at Soho Square is always capable of dealing a poisoned blow.

A Tale of Two Cities is a tale of two heroes. The theme of the double has such obvious attractions for a writer preoccupied with disguises, rival impulses, and hidden affinities that it is surprising that Dickens didn't make more use of it elsewhere. But no one could claim that his handling of the device is very successful here, or that he has managed to range the significant forces of the novel behind Carton and Darnay. Darnay is, so to speak, the accredited representative of Dickens in the novel, the 'normal' hero for whom a happy ending is still possible. It has been noted, interestingly enough, that he shares his creator's initials—and that is pretty well the only interesting thing about him. Otherewise he is a pasteboard character, completely undeveloped. His position as an exile, his struggles as a language-teacher, his admiration for George Washington are so many openings thrown away.

Carton, of course, is a far more striking figure. He belongs to the line of cultivated wastrels who play an increasingly large part in Dickens's novels during the second half of his career, culminating in Eugene Wrayburn; his clearest predecessor, as his name indicates, is the luckless Richard Carstone of *Bleak House*. He has squandered his gifts and drunk away his early promise; his will is broken, but his intellect is unimpaired. In a sense, his opposite is not Darnay at all, but the aggressive Stryver, who makes a fortune by picking his brains. Yet there is something hollow about his complete resignation to failure: his self-abasement in front of Lucie, for instance. ('I am like one who died young . . . I know very well that you can have no tenderness for me . . .') For, stagy a figure though he is, Carton does suggest what Thomas Hardy calls 'fearful unfulfilments'; he still has vitality, and it is hard to believe that he has gone down without a struggle. The total effect is one of energy held unnaturally in check: the bottled-up frustration which Carton represents must spill over somewhere.

Carton's and Darnay's fates are entwined from their first meeting, at the Old Bailey trial. Over the dock there hangs a mirror: 'crowds of the wicked and the wretched had been reflected in it, and had passed from its surface and this earth's together. Haunted in a most ghastly manner that abominable place would have been, if the glass could ever have rendered back its reflections, as the ocean is one day to give up its dead.' (Bk. II, Ch. 2.) After Darnay's acquittal we leave him with Carton, 'so like each other in feature, so unlike in manner, both reflected in the glass above them'. Reflections, like ghosts, suggest unreality and self-division, and at the end of the same day Carton stares at his own image in the glass and upbraids it: 'Why should you particularly like a man who resembles you? There is nothing in you to like: you know that. Ah, confound you! . . . Come on, and have it out in plain words! You hate the fellow.' (Bk. II, Ch. 4.) In front of the mirror, Carton thinks of changing places with Darnay; at the end of the book, he is to take the other's death upon him. Dickens prepares the ground:

when Darnay is in jail, it is Carton who strikes Mr. Lorry as having 'the wasted air of a prisoner', and when he is visited by Carton on the rescue attempt, he thinks at first that he is 'an apparition of his own imagining'. But Dickens is determined to stick by Darnay: a happy ending *must* be possible. As Lorry and his party gallop to safety with the drugged Darnay, there is an abrupt switch to the first person: 'The wind is rushing after us, and the clouds are flying after us, and the moon is plunging after us, and the whole wild night is in pursuit of us; but so far, we are pursued by nothing else.' (Bk. III, Ch. 13.) *We* can make our escape, however narrowly; Carton, expelled from our system, must be abandoned to his fate.

But the last word is with Carton—the most famous last word in Dickens, in fact. Those who take a simplified view of Dickens's radicalism, or regard him as one of nature's Marxists, can hardly help regretting that *A Tale of Two Cities* should end as it does. They are bound to feel, with Edgar Johnson, that 'instead of merging, the truth of revolution and the truth of sacrifice are made to appear in conflict'. A highly personal, indeed a unique crisis cuts across public issues and muffles the political message. But this is both to sentimentalize Dickens's view of the revolution, and to miss the point about Carton. The cynical judgment that his sacrifice was trifling, since he had nothing to live for, is somewhat nearer the mark. Drained of the will to live, he is shown in the closing chapters of the book as a man courting death, and embracing it when it comes. 'In seasons of pestilence, some of us will have a secret attraction to the disease—a terrible passing inclination to die of it. And all of us have like wonders hidden in our breasts, only needing circumstances to evoke them.' (Bk. III, Ch. 6.) It is Carton rather than Darnay who is 'drawn to the loadstone rock'.[1] On his last walk around Paris, a passage which Shaw cites in the preface to *Man and Superman* as proof of Dickens's essentially irreligious nature, his thoughts run on religion: 'I am the Resurrection and the Life.' But his impressions are all of death: the day comes coldly, 'looking like a dead face out of the sky', while on the river 'a trading boat, with a sail of the softened colour of a dead leaf, then glided into his view, floated by him, and died away'. (Bk. III, Ch. 9.) His walk recalls an earlier night, when he wandered round London with 'wreaths of dust spinning round and round before the morning blast, as if the desert sand had risen far away and the first spray of it in its advance had begun to overwhelm the city'. (Bk. II, Ch. 5.) Then, with the wilderness bringing home to him a sense of the wasted powers within him, he saw a momentary mirage of what he might have achieved and was reduced to tears; but now that the city has been overwhelmed in earnest, he is past thinking of what might have been. 'It is a far, far better thing that I do, than I have ever done'—but the 'better thing' might just as well be committing suicide as laying down his life for Darnay. At any rate, he thinks of himself as going towards rest, not towards resurrection.

By this time the revolution has become simply the agency of death, the storm that overwhelms the city. Or rather, all the pent-up fury and resentment that is allowed no outlet in the 'personal' side of the book, with Carton kow-towing to Stryver and nobly renouncing Lucie, boils over in revolutionary violence: Dickens dances the Carmagnole, and howls for blood with the mob. Frightened by the forces which he has released, he views the revolution with hatred and disgust; he doesn't record a single incident in which it might be shown as beneficent, constructive or even tragic. Instead, it is described time and again in terms of pestilence and madness. Dickens will hear nothing of noble aspirations; the disorder of the whole period is embodied in the dervishes who dance the Carmagnole—'no fight could have been half so terrible'. Confronted with the crowd, Dickens reaches for his gun; he looks into eyes 'which any unbrutalized beholder would have given twenty years of life, to have petrified with a well-directed gun'. (Bk. III, Ch. 2.) That 'well-directed' has the true ring of outraged rate-paying respectability, while the image seems oddly out of place in a book which has laid so much stress on the stony faces and petrified hearts of the aristocracy.

Dickens can only deal with mob-violence in a deliberately picturesque story set in the past. But *A Tale of Two Cities*, written by a middle-aged man who could afford a longer perspective at a time when Chartism was already receding into history, is not quite analogous to *Barnaby Rudge*. There, however contemptible we are meant to find the world of Sir John Chester, the riots are an explosion of madness and nothing more. But the French Revolution compels Dickens to acquire a theory of history, however primitive: 'crush humanity out of shape once more, under similar hammers, and it will twist itself into the same tortured forms'. (Bk III, Ch. 15.) The revolutionaries return evil for evil; the guillotine is the product not of innate depravity but of intolerable oppression. If Dickens's sympathies shift towards the aristocrats as soon as they become victims, he can also show a grim restraint; he underlines the horror of Foulon's death, strung up with a bunch of grass tied to his back (how his imagination pounces on such a detail!), but he never allows us to forget who Foulon was. Nor does he have any sympathy with those who talk of the Revolution 'as though it were the only harvest under the skies that had never been sown', although he himself is at times plainly tempted to treat it as an inexplicable calamity, a rising of the sea (the gaoler at La Force has the bloated body of a drowned man, and so forth) or a rising of fire: the flames which destroy the château of St. Evrémonde 'blow from the infernal regions', convulsing nature until the lead boils over inside the stone fountains. But cause and effect are never kept out of sight for long; Dickens is always reminding himself that the Revolution, though 'a frightful moral disorder', was born of 'unspeakable suffering, intolerable oppression, and heartless indifference'. Society was diseased before the fever broke out: the shattered cask of wine which at the outset falls on the 'crippling' stones of Saint Antoine is scooped up in little mugs of 'mutilated' earthenware.

But to grasp a patient's medical history is not to condone his disease, and Dickens is unyielding in his hostility to the crowd. The buzzing of the flies on the scent for carrion at the Old Bailey trial and the mass-rejoicing at Roger Cly's funeral are early indications of what he feels. The courtroom in Paris is also full of buzzing and stirring, but by this time the atmosphere has become positively cannibalistic; a jury of dogs has been empanelled to try the deer, Madame Defarge 'feasts' on the prisoner, Jacques III, with his very Carlylean croak, is described as an epicure.

Whatever Dickens's motives, a good deal of this is no doubt perfectly valid; morbid fantasies can still prompt shrewd observations, as when we are shown Darnay, the prisoner of half an hour, already learning to count the steps as he is led away to his cell. In particular, Dickens recognizes the ways in which a period of upheaval can obliterate the individual personality; there is no more telling detail in the book than the roll-call of the condemned containing the names of a prisoner who has died in jail and two who have already been guillotined, all of them forgotten. Insane suspicion, senseless massacres, the rise to power of the worst elements: in the era of Gladstonian budgets Dickens understands the workings of a police state.

But it would be ludicrous to claim very much for the accuracy of Dickens's account of the French Revolution as such. There are scarcely any references to the actual course of events, and no suggestion at all that the revolution had an intellectual or idealistic content, while the portrayal of fanaticism seems childish if we compare it even with something as one-sided as *The Gods are Athirst*. For the purposes of the novel, the revolution is the Defarges, and although Carton foresees that Defarge in his turn will perish on the guillotine, he has no inkling of how the whole internecine process will ever come to a halt. As for Madame Defarge, she is as much driven by fate as the stony-hearted Marquis, with his coachmen cracking their whips like the Furies: the time has laid 'a dreadfully disfiguring hand upon her'. Her last entry is her most dramatic. Miss Pross is bathing her eyes to rid herself of feverish apprehensions, when she suddenly appears—materializes, one might say—in the doorway:

> The basin fell to the ground broken, and the water flowed to the feet of Madame Defarge. By strange stern ways, and through much staining blood, those feet had come to meet that water. (Bk. III, Ch. 14.)

We are reminded, by rather too forcible a contrast, of the broken cask of red wine which prefaces Madame Defarge's first appearance in the novel. Her element, from the very start, is blood.

Still, *A Tale of Two Cities* is not a private nightmare, but a work which continues to give pleasure. Dickens's drives and conflicts are his raw material, not the source of his artistic power, and in itself the fact that the novel twists the French Revolution into a highly personal fantasy proves nothing: so, after all, does *The Scarlet Pimpernel.* Everything depends on the quality of the writing—which is usually one's cue, in talking about Dickens, to pay tribute to his exuberance and fertility. Dickens's genius inheres in minute particulars; later we may discern patterns of symbolism and imagery, a design which lies deeper than the plot, but first we are struck by the lavish heaping-up of acute observations, startling similes, descriptive flourishes, circumstantial embroidery. Or such is the case with every Dickens novel except for the *Tale,* which is written in a style so grey and unadorned that many readers are reluctant to grant it a place in the Canon at all. Dickens wouldn't be Dickens if there weren't occasional touches like the 'hospital procession of negro cupids, several headless and all cripples', which Mr. Lorry notices framing the mirror in his hotel (or the whitewashed cupid 'in the coolest linen' on the ceiling of his Paris office, which makes its appearance three hundred pages later). But for the most part one goes to the book for qualities which are easier to praise than to illustrate or examine: a rapid tempo which never lets up from the opening sentence, and a sombre eloquence which saves Carton from mere melodrama, and stamps an episode like the running-down of the child by the Marquis's carriage on one's mind with a primitive intensity rarely found after Dickens's early novels, like an outrage committed in a fairy-tale.

But it must be admitted that the *Tale* is in many ways a thin and uncharacteristic work, bringing the mounting despair of the eighteen-fifties to a dead end rather than ushering in the triumphs of the 'sixties. In no other novel, not even *Hard Times,* has Dickens's natural profusion been so drastically pruned. Above all, the book is notoriously deficient in humour. One falls—or flops—back hopefully on the Crunchers, but to small avail. True, the comic element parodies the serious action: Jerry, like his master, is a 'Resurrection-Man', but on the only occasion that we see him rifling a grave it turns out to be empty, while his son's panic-stricken flight with an imaginary coffin in full pursuit is nightmarish rather than funny. As comic characters the Crunchers are forced and mechanical; such true humour as there is in the book is rather to be found in scattered observations, but settings and characters are colourful rather than grotesque. Obviously Dickens's humour is many things, but it is usually bound up with a sense of almost magical power over nature: to distort, exaggerate, yoke together or dissolve is to manipulate and control external reality. In

Dickens people are always taking on the qualities of objects with which they come into contact, and *vice versa*: a basic Dickensian trick of style, which makes its appearance as early as the opening pages of *Sketches by Boz*, where there is a fine passage ('Our Parish', Chapter VII) on the 'resemblance and sympathy' between a man's face and the knocker on his front door. Such transformations are not unknown in *A Tale of Two Cities*—there is the obstinate door at Tellson's with the weak rattle in its throat, for example—but they occur less frequently than in any other Dickens novel, and there is a corresponding lack of power for which a neatly constructed plot is small compensation.

Contrary to what might be expected, this absence of burlesque is accompanied by a failure to present society in any depth. *A Tale of Two Cities* may deal with great political events, but nowhere else in the later work of Dickens is there less sense of society as a living organism. Evrémondes and Defarges alike seem animated by sheer hatred; we hear very little of the stock social themes, money, hypocrisy, and snobbery. Tellson's, musty and cramped and antiquated, makes an excellent Dickensian set-piece, but it is scarcely followed up. Jarvis Lorry, too, is a sympathetic version of the fairy-godfather, a saddened Cheeryble who repines at spending his days 'turning a vast pecuniary mangle', but this side of his character is only lightly sketched in. He may glance through the iron bars of his office-window 'as if they were ruled for figures too, and everything under the clouds were a sum', but he is more important as a protective, reassuring figure: in times of revolution Tellson's mustiness becomes a positive virtue.

The lack of social density shows up Dickens's melodrama to disadvantage. This is partly a question of length, since in a short novel everything has to be worked in as best it can: Barsad will inevitably turn out to be Miss Pross's long-lost brother, Defarge has to double as Doctor Manette's old servant, and so forth. But there is a deeper reason for feeling more dissatisfaction with the artificial plot here than one does with equally far-fetched situations elsewhere in Dickens. Where society is felt as an all-enveloping force, Dickens is able to turn the melodramatic conventions which he inherited to good use; however preposterous the individual coincidences, they serve an important symbolic function. The world is more of a piece than we suppose, Dickens is saying, and our fates are bound up, however cut off from one another we may appear: the pestilence from Tom-all-Alone's really will spread to the Dedlock mansion, and sooner or later the river in which Gaffer Hexam fishes for corpses will flow through the Veneering drawing-room. In a word, we can't have Miss Havisham without Magwitch. But without a thick social atmosphere swirling round them, the characters of *A Tale of Two Cities* stand out in stark melodramatic isolation; the spotlight is trained too sharply on the implausibilities of the plot, and the stage is set for Sir John Martin-Harvey and *The Only Way*. So, too, the relentless workings of destiny are stressed rather clumsily by such a bare presentation; Madame Defarge points the finger of fate a little too vigorously, and there is a tendency towards heavy repetitions and parallelisms, brought out by the chapter-headings, 'A Hand at Cards' and 'The Game Made', 'Dusk' and 'Darkness', and so forth.

Yet despite the dark mood in which it was conceived, the *Tale* isn't a wholly gloomy work; nor is the final impression which it leaves with us one of a wallow of self-pity on the scaffold. We are told of Darnay in the condemned cell (or is it Carton?) that

> his hold on life was strong, and it was very, very hard to loosen; by gradual efforts and degrees unclosed a little here, it clenched the tighter there; and when he brought his strength to bear on that hand and it yielded, this was closed again. There was a hurry, too, in all his thoughts, a turbulent and heated working of his heart, that contended against resignation. (Bk. III, Ch. 13.)

And near the end, as Miss Pross grapples with Madame Defarge, Dickens speaks of 'the vigorous tenacity of love, always so much stronger than hate'. The gruesome events of the book scarcely bear out such a judgment, yet as an article of faith, if not as a statement of the literal truth, it is curiously impressive. For all the sense of horror which he must have felt stirring within him when he wrote *A Tale of Two Cities*, Dickens remained a moralist and a preacher, and it was his saving strength. But if the author doesn't succumb with Carton, neither does he escape with Darnay. At the end of the book 'we' gallop away not to safety and Lucie, but to the false hopes of Pip, the thwarted passion of Bradley Headstone, the divided life of John Jasper. Nothing is concluded, and by turning his malaise into a work of art Dickens obtains parole, not release: the prison will soon be summoning him once more.

---

[1]Darnay, who only comes to life in the face of death, is nevertheless obsessed with the guillotine. He has 'a strange besetting desire to know what to do when the time came, a desire gigantically disproportionate to the few swift moments to which it referred; a wondering that was more like the wondering of some other spirit within his, than his own'. (Bk. III, Ch. 13.) Carton's spirit, perhaps; through the exigencies of the plot, Dickens has got the wires crossed.

Selected Criticisms

In the *Tale of Two Cities,* Mr. Dickens . . . has put before his readers dishes of which the quality is not disguised by the cooking. . . . It [the book] has the merit of being much shorter than its predecessors and the consequence is, that the satisfaction which both the author and his readers must feel at its conclusion was deferred for a considerably less period than usual.

Sir James Fitzjames Stephen

I should myself prefer to say that its [the book's] distinctive merit is less in any of its conceptions of character, even Carton's, than as a specimen of Dicken's power in imaginative story-telling. There is no piece of fiction known to me, in which the domestic life of a few simple private people is in such a manner knitted and interwoven with the outbreak of a terrible public event, that the one seems but part of the other. When made conscious of the first sultry drops of a thunderstorm that fall upon a little group sitting in an obscure English lodging, we are witness to the actual beginning of a tempest which is preparing to sweep away everything in France. And, to the end, the book in this respect is really remarkable.

John Forster

A Tale of Two Cities is not tragedy; it is not shapely, profound, and austere. But it is a powerful story; and the culminating scene, when Sydney Carton atones for a misspent life by his act of self-immolation, is nobly conceived and has made many a heart beat. The subordinate figures, the young aristocrat who owes his life to Carton's devotion, the heroine, the bloodthirsty revolutionaries, Madame Defarge and the rest of the women of the Terror, are creatures of melodrama which he [Dickens] did his best to authenticate from such books as he had time to read and from other sources. But his own recollections of the days of mail-coaches and diligences, of an era, that is, which was that of many episodes in his other novels, and all that he had seen with his own eyes in his many sojourns in France, served him well enough in such incidental pictures as of the mail going over Shooter's Hill, the Royal George Hotel at Dover, the quiet sanctum of Tellson's bank, and the closing scene, the flight from Paris.

Ernest A. Baker

A Tale of Two Cities has been hailed as the best of Dickens's books and damned as the worst. It is neither, but it is certainly in some ways the least characteristic, and that fact explains the divergent opinions of it.

Edgar Johnson

Certain critics have also tried to make out that there is a special political significance in the fact that Dickens chose to write about the French Revolution. Yet, although it is true that Dickens actually believed in the possibility of a vast uprising in England, if the state refused to listen to the just demands of 'working-men', he kept to the main theme of the story with sound judgement and without glancing back. The whole novel has too great a general significance for it to be profitable to try to isolate personal opinions.

K. J. Fielding

The greatest imaginative energy of *A Tale of Two Cities* is suggested, by a title, once more, that Dickens considered and rejected: "Buried Alive". His only great hope for the 'frightful moral disorder' of the world lay, imaginatively if not doctrinally, in some kind of moral and vital regeneration, and the reiterated and varied playing on themes of regeneration and resurrection in *A Tale of Two Cities* provides the strongest line of imaginative coherence in this too often superficial novel.

Monroe Engel

The book is not *War and Peace*. His tale remains the account of one small group of characters who suffered in the course of the cataclysm which surged about them and went on to historical, political, and economic developments completely beyond the purposes of the tale. On a small and relatively selective scale within the limits defined it is a dynamic historical novel, even though it does not call upon all the technical resources at Dickens' command. He sacrificed solidity for the spectacular, the large scene for the single vivid flash, but he got it.

Earle Davis

Dickens was, in his way, a great artist, but he was never a pure artist. Aspects of his mind, interesting in themselves, but structurally irrelevant, are always liable to break in. But sometimes . . . we can have the satisfaction of feeling that the imperfections contribute to the making of later and better works.

. . .

In *A Tale of Two Cities*, he contrived to give a keener impression of an invisible crowd, of mounting communal passions nursed in secret which must one day overthrow the government. Dickens had little of importance to say about the meaning of political revolution. But he was able, especially by the use of images of darkness, to convey a fine glimpse of slowly nurtured social forces coming to catastrophic fruition.

. . .

Vulgar in his tastes, and towering in his imagination, Dickens seized eagerly upon the ridiculous paraphernalia of English melodrama. He enjoyed over-obvious comparisons, like the wine running through the gutters and foreshadowing the blood bath of the Revolution in *A Tale of Two Cities*.

A. O. J. Cockshut

What Dickens planned in *A Tale of Two Cities* was, as he told John Forster, 'a picaresque story, rising in every chapter with characters true to nature, but whom the story should express, more than they should express themselves in dialogue.' It was to be a story of incident, in other words, a story for the story's sake; when he had finished it, he 'hoped' it was the best story he had written, and, taken as a story, there can be no doubt that it is.

. . .

The only fair test for the quality of *A Tale of Two Cities* is . . . whether it achieves successfully what Dickens set out to do. My judgment upon that point I must give frankly for what it is worth. I do not believe that *A Tale of Two Cities* scales the frozen heights of tragic grandeur . . . but I do believe that it is a fascinating and deeply moving story which must take a very high rank indeed among productions of the second rank.

. . .

A Tale of Two Cities is one of the most famous of all historical novels, but it is an historical novel in a very special sense. . . . Dickens has not historical personages in the foreground, nor in the background either. . . . The method is pictorial as well as dramatic. . . . The whole book is seen like that; it has a vivid cinematic quality about it. [Of sentimentality and melodrama, two traditional charges against Dickens:] I find sentiment but not sentimentality in the touching scene at the end between Carton and the seamstress. . . . As for the culminating act in the novel, Carton's sacrifice, it undoubtedly appeals to the softer emotions, yet in some aspects Carton may fairly be described as a very unsentimental character. . . . The chapter in which Miss Pross kills Madame Defarge was criticized as melodramatic . . . strictly speaking, it is more sensational than melodramatic. . . .

Edward Wagenknecht

[*A Tale of Two Cities* was] popular yet somewhat mechanical . . . [and in addition, Dickens] made the experiment of subduing . . . comic extravagances by reducing dialogue and comic relief to a minimum. The results were disappointing, and he was happy to return to his more characteristic manner. . . .

George Ford

Dickens had easy graphic power, wonderfully minute observation.

His literary method is that of all great novelists. To set before his readers the image so vivid in his own mind, he simply describes and reports. We have, in general, a very precise and complete picture of externals—the face, the gesture, the habit. In this Dickens excels; he proves to us by sheer force of visible detail, how actual was the mental form from which he drew. We learn the tone of voice, the trick of utterance; he declared that every word spoken by his characters was audible to him. . . . We know these people because we see and hear them.

George Gissing

The one thing that everyone who has read *A Tale of Two Cities* remembers is the Reign of Terror. The whole book is dominated by the guillotine—tumbrils thundering to and fro, bloody knives, heads bouncing into the basket, and sinister old women knitting as they watch. Actually these scenes only occupy a few chapters, but they are written with terrible intensity, and the rest of the book is rather slow going. . . . Dickens sees clearly enough that the French Revolution was bound to happen . . . the revolutionaries appear to him simply as degraded savages—in fact, as lunatics. . . . The apologists of any revolution generally try to minimize its horrors; Dickens' impulse is to exaggerate them—and from a historical point of view he had certainly exaggerated.

George Orwell

Dickens could understand [the Revolution] for he was simple and not subtle. He understood that plain rage against plain political injustice; he understood again that vindictiveness and that obvious brutality which followed . . . his description of the city he did not know is almost better than his description of the city he did know. . . .

G. K. Chesterton

It is one of the many charges levelled in disparagement against Dickens' later novels—as compared with his earlier ones—that his plots "grew more mysterious." A generation which has witnessed the rise of the detective novel to the place it occupies to-day, can hardly see in this "mysteriousness" a blemish. The truth is that Dickens, always a workman, paid the greatest possible attention to the construction of his novels. If in his earlier novels he scattered "characters" with a reckless profusion, in his later works he is at infinite pains to bring on the stage only just so many characters as have actual work to do. His devoted "public" combined with his natural genius, made it imperative that he should bring on to his stage a fuller parade of characters than most novelists would care to try to control. And the fact also that his novels all appeared in parts or in instalments made it imperative that his every part or instalment should contain its specially outstanding incident. Few, if any, writers ever attempted so difficult a task as Dickens did every time he tackled the job of making a large crowd work as a team and weaving a whole hierarchy of main and subsidiary plots and counterplots into a perfectly reticulated whole. And Dickens' skill in this direction was seldom shown to finer advantage than in the *Tale of Two Cities*. . . .

Most emphatic of all, as an indication of Dickens' standpoint and bias, is his conception of Sidney Carton. That which is usually lost upon readers of the *Tale of Two Cities* and a point which disappears entirely in the dramatized version (for which, of course, Dickens is not responsible), is the fact that the resemblance between Carton and Darnay—which makes possible Carton's substitution-sacrifice—does not end at a mere external physical likeness. Both are attracted by, and fall wholly in love with Lucie Manette, and both possess the same reckless generosity and readiness for sacrifice in a worthy cause which in the end leads Carton to take his heroic "only way" out of Lucie's terrible crisis.

Before Carton makes his sacrifice, Darnay has made his. He has sacrificed his title and his inheritance from a sense of their essential injustice and as the only recompense at his command for the wrong these things—titles and feudal rights and privileges—have entailed. Moreover, he has imperilled his personal safety and indeed, his life, to respond to the appeal for protection from a faithful servant, in peril in consequence of doing his duty. Darnay's large-hearted generosity and self-sacrifice precede and create the occasion (as well as the need) for Carton's ultimate self-sacrifice.

Thus by a whole succession of strokes Dickens makes the resemblance between Carton and Darnay extend from their outward appearance to their fundamental character.

There is, of course, an obvious difference. Darnay is as sober and careful as Carton is drunken and careless. In these regards they are opposites. But—and this is usually overlooked—the same contempt of himself which makes Carton a failure and a drunkard is also the quality which makes him prompt to seize the "only way" out of Lucie's difficulties. Thus his supreme virtue has one and the same root as his chief vice.

Dickens here shows, as he often does, his addiction to the doctrine of Robert Owen: "man's character is made *for* him, and not *by* him." With a little difference in their upbringing and their circumstances, Darnay would have been the failure and the drunkard, and Carton the sober and well-conducted husband. The turn of a hair at a critical stage was enough to separate their respective paths in life, so that their opposition in outward seeming is an expression of the fundamental identity of their characters. Carton is to Darnay and Darnay to Carton only another instance of the great truth: "There, but for the grace of circumstances outside my control, go I!"

That Dickens intends this moral to be drawn is clear from any number of strokes. When Darnay and Carton first meet Carton behaves insolently—behaves, as he admits to himself, as though he hated Darnay because he shows him, concretely, what he himself might have been. Later on, after Lucie and Darnay are married their children show a special fondness for Carton. The soundness of an unspoiled child's instincts is one of Dickens' favourite themes.

Nothing is said about Carton's childhood; but from his complete lack of relatives and connections in his manhood it would seem that his parents must have died while he was still an infant. In Darnay's case we know that he was prepared for the sacrifice of his title and his estates by the teaching of his mother—who felt that so cruel had been the injustices worked in their name that there was a curse upon both. It seems a fair inference, and one quite in keeping with Dickens' usual mode of reasoning to suppose that Carton's habitual lack of self-respect or self-regard came from an early training in which he was treated as of no account.

It will be remembered that the theme of a thoroughly good-natured and generous lad, sinking, through lack of proper self-regard, and of any purpose in life, into a drifter, and finally a waster and sot, was one that Dickens had experimented with before. Jingle was nearly in this class, but was rescued from it by a native streak of roguery. Dick Swiveller was clearly a case in point, until he was saved by his discovery of the Marchioness, his illness and the opportune death (and legacy) of his aunt. Steerforth is not of this class; he is too much of a fine-gentleman, too lacking in real generosity, not fond enough of drink, and altogether too fond of himself to qualify. But, as we noted above, Walter, in *Dombey*, was intended to be of this order, until Dickens relented.

With Sidney Carton, therefore, Dickens was able, at last, to work out a theme which he had been wanting for years to work out—the theme of the good man gone wrong through lack of the ballast necessary to compensate for sheer excess of good-nature. It is a theme which, quite clearly, shows the bent of Dickens' mind to have been in the direction of the Helvetius-Owen doctrine of the moral equality of man, and the general perfectability of human-nature. And from this doctrine, as Marx and Engels showed, Communism is a logical deduction.

In sum: the *Tale of Two Cities* takes, as clearly as its predecessors had done, the side of the common people against that of the privileged classes. But it adds, more plainly than any of its predecessors, a warning of an Avenging Fate, from fear of which all the privileged, and all those set in authority, would do well to reconsider their ways.

T. A. Jackson

Review Questions and Answers

Question 1.

What is the significance of setting in this novel? How do the "two cities" themselves contribute to the action and plot?

Answer

The novel is literally a tale about two cities and the inhabitants of both. Dickens shows the reader the temper of English mobs as well as French mobs. He indicates that the difference between the anticipation of a hideous execution by the Old Bailey crowd at Charles Darnay's London trial and the thirst for blood by the French courtroom spectators is only one of degree. Dickens presents the English judicial system as well as the French Revolutionary one. We see the England of the late eighteenth century and we see the atmosphere of its French counterpart. In short, we see the people and the attitudes of two cities, separated by a narrow body of water, the English Channel. The action of the book can be regarded as a periodic movement from one of these points to the other. Lucie Manette and Jarvis Lorry come from England to rescue Dr. Manette from his room over Defarge's wineshop and take him back to England. Charles Darnay had travelled back and forth from England to France before his first trial at the Old Bailey. Jarvis Lorry had come to Paris on Tellson's business, since the banking house maintained offices in both that city and London. Charles Darnay's imprisonment brings Dr. Manette, Lucie, and her child to Paris to assist him if they can. When Darnay's plight seems hopeless at his return to prison, Sydney Carton crosses from London to Paris. Several of the characters themselves share double identities and the blood of two nationalities as well. Charles Darnay, the English tutor, is the Marquis D'Evrémonde. Solomon Pross is also John Barsad, the Old Bailey spy, as well as one of the French prison sheep. Lucie herself is the daughter of a French father and an English mother, and the blood of both countries flows through the veins of little Lucie too.

For the central characters, one city represents danger, while the other provides safety. Both cities stand as separate poles in the book's structure, and yet both are united in the Darnays, Alexander Manette and his daughter, Lucie. *A Tale of Two Cities* is therefore a tale of two nations, with the cities acting as anchors for the plot.

Question 2.

Discuss Dickens' use of structural detail.

Answer

In analyzing the structure of this novel, one immediately recognizes the infinite amount of narrative detail that Dickens has woven into the development of the plot. Jerry Cruncher's mysterious occupation is a fine example of the author's use of structural details. Jerry's boots often had mud on them in the mornings, even though his job as Tellson's messenger did not call for muddy work. Young Jerry was puzzled about the rust on his father's fingers when they never encountered rust during his messenger chores. Jerry himself said that he went fishing at night and that he was an "honest tradesman." He had an extraordinary interest in funerals and even left his spot outside Tellson's to follow Cly's coffin to the grave. He often remarked that if coming back to life became popular, he would be in a bad way. In addition, there is also the matter of his wife's flopping and praying against the success of his mysterious work.

These are examples of the author's use of detail as a unifying force. Such a connective tissue of detail contributes suspense but, more importantly, a structural cohesion in the novel when the mysterious aspects are finally cleared away. Actually, Dickens' structural details accomplish something beyond simple narrative unity: they periodically impel the action of the story. To use the Jerry Cruncher example once again, Jerry's discovery that Barsad and Cly had faked Cly's death and burial works to Charles Darnay's advantage, for Sydney Carton uses the information to help force Barsad into assisting in Darnay's escape from prison. Certainly, a substantial part of Dickens' art must be recognized as this ability to create an incredible structural web, one that is carefully controlled throughout the novel, and that weaves event and action into a seamless whole. It can be said that Dickens is a master of interrelation, a process which commences at the book's beginning, grows steadily as the plot develops, and accomplishes a resolution of all loose ends by the final chapter.

Question 3.
How did serialization affect the structure of the novel?

Answer
Dickens' novels were serialized, that is, they appeared in monthly instalments in magazines. A novel not written for serialization often adapts poorly to a piecemeal presentation, while a work written specifically for instalment presentation may not appear unified when issued as a single volume. One of the effects of serialization upon a novel is the creation of a more episodic structure. *A Tale of Two Cities* contains chapters that are simultaneously self-contained and anticipatory. What we have referred to as narrative threads are closely related to the success of serialized publication, for what they accomplish is the unification of chapter units published over many months' time. If a sense of coincidence and contrivance seems to tax the credibility of the reader at times, it must be realized that such qualities are potent unifiers in the periodical publication of a long

book. The appearances of John Barsad and his relationship to other characters have a strong coincidental flavor about them. He is Miss Pross' brother. He is an Old Bailey witness against Darnay, and he accidentally meets Miss Pross in Paris after years of separation. He *happens* to meet Sydney Carton at the same moment. He *happens* to be the single mourner following the coffin that Jerry discovers is empty. He *happens* to be the spy in the Saint Antoine quarter. He *happens* to reveal to the Defarges that Lucie Manette was to marry the nephew of the Marquis D'Evrémonde, and he *happens* to be a prison sheep in the fortress where Darnay is held before he is to be executed.

In a lesser writer, such coincidence would pall heavily on the reader. However, Dickens is a splendid storyteller; and if appearing too episodic and too contrived at times, he is masterful in the basic richness of a story line that carries with it a full command of event and development.

Question 4.

Discuss the overall sense of balance in *A Tale of Two Cities.*

Answer

The structural balance in the novel can be seen in such areas as the division of action between the "two cities," several examples of parallel events, and in the rises and falls of the characters' fortunes. London and Paris serve as the two locales for the novel, with the action moving back and forth between them. There are several examples where a social condition or an episode occurring in one of the two cities differs from a parallel circumstance in the other only in the matter of degree. The mock funeral of Cly, at which a weighted coffin is buried, finds a parallel in the mock funeral of the old aristocrat, Foulon, who, like Cly, wished to be thought dead. Charles Darnay stands trial in both France and England, and Dickens provides alternate glimpses of the French and English peoples. Many are slaughtered for frivolous reasons and imaginary crimes in the frenzy of the Revolution, but Dickens indicates that even so honorable an institution as Tellson's "had taken so many lives [in the course of its business] that, if the heads laid low before it were ranged on Temple Bar instead of being privately disposed of, they would probably have excluded what little light the ground floor had, in a rather significant manner."

With the gradual rise of Sydney Carton in the novel, there is a gradual and parallel decline in the fortunes of Charles Darnay. With an increase in the ability of Carton to assist Darnay, there is a parallel weakening in the capability of Dr. Manette to do so. The gentle strength of Miss Pross is balanced in the book by the vicious force of Madame Defarge. In the moment of struggle between these two characters, Dickens represents the meeting of love and hate in a final combat for the lives of the Darnays and Dr. Manette. And, indeed, the majority of the characters in *A Tale of Two Cities* can be ranged either on the side of love or that of hate. Lucie and Charles Darnay, Dr. Manette, Miss Pross, Sydney Carton and Jarvis Lorry are obviously motivated by love, affection, and tender loyalties. The Defarges (with an occasional lapse into reason and humanitarianism by Ernest Defarge), The Vengeance, Jacques Three, the mender of roads and the mobs of the Revolution stand opposed to these qualities.

Question 5.
How do Dickens' minor characters contribute to the narrative development?

Answer
In *A Tale of Two Cities,* Jarvis Lorry and Miss Pross are fine examples of Dickens' use of minor characters to advance the action of the novel. Jarvis Lorry never contributes significantly to the story but attends to what can be called the necessary details that allow the more important action to proceed without obstruction. He is the one who brings the news of Lucie's father to her at the beginning of the book, and he is also the person who makes the arrangement for the escape by coach when Charles Darnay is smuggled out of prison. Miss Pross, like Jarvis Lorry, acts as something of a custodian and guardian spirit for the Darnays and Dr. Manette. However, her relationship to Solomon Pross-John Barsad is important, for it opens the way for Sydney Carton to force Barsad's participation in his plan to save Charles Darnay. It is Miss Pross who, as much as Carton, and in her own way, saves the Darnays and Dr. Manette when she battles Madame Defarge to the death. Neither Miss Pross nor Mr. Lorry loom as major characters, but their contributions to the development of the novel are significant.

Question 6.
Is there a variety of motivations behind the action of the characters in the novel?

Answer
The motivations of the characters in *A Tale* are generally uncomplicated. Love, hate, revenge, loyalty, self-sacrifice, humanitarianism, and patriotism are all apparent in the characters. Sydney Carton is really the only figure who offers any complexity of motivation. He loves Lucie, and this is basic to his sacrifice. But there is really more to Carton's act than this. His life has been a waste. He has dissipated his talent and potential; and far from enjoying his excesses, he has suffered considerably from them. The loudest and most reproachful voice that tells him this, other than Stryver's, is Carton's own. He fully realizes his condition and the futility of the life that remains ahead of him. The plan to save Charles Darnay provides

Carton with the opportunity of doing two significant things. Initially, his self-sacrifice will give his love for Lucie the one visible expression it can ever have. In addition, his own death will save the life of another human being, a man whom Carton looks upon as infinitely finer than himself. The first aspect of his motivation is of a truly spiritual nature, for the sacrifice will produce the resurrection of the man himself. It will give value to his otherwise worthless life. It will make all the personal frustration and failure pale before that final act and will allow those long years of decline to represent nothing more than a poor prelude to a sublime act of selflessness. Carton's desire for redemption must, therefore, be recognized as a potent motivating force along with that of his fine and tender love for Lucie.

Question 7.

Does any single tonal quality persist in *A Tale of Two Cities*?

Answer

Those sections of the novel that contain Dickens' social criticism are bitterly sarcastic. The very first chapter of the book is a splendid example of this when Dickens uses a biting tone in describing conditions in both England and France. Chapter 7 of the second book, "Monseigneur in Town," is an instance of the author's sharpest and bitterest thrusts at a shallow, impotent and useless aristocracy. Rather than employ direct attack, Dickens uses a droll sarcasm that politely and, in a manner of quiet dignity, devastates the aristocratic class and exposes its degeneracy and fatal weakness to the reader.

Question 8.

Discuss Dickens' dramatic sense as an important aspect of his style.

Answer

We know of Dickens' great affinity for the theater. He had an eye for the dramatic and he was able to incorporate in *A Tale* many scenes that are truly the work of a dramatist, a man who is conscious of stage setting, of the effects of lighting and of the particular way an audience focusses its attention on a scene. At Charles Darnay's trial in the Old Bailey, the reader witnesses the progress of the courtroom scene as if he were one of the spectators who had crowded in along with the rest of the mob. The broken wine-cask scene before Defarge's shop and the grindstone episode in the courtyard of Tellson's Paris office are both dramatically conceived. Both scenes seem suddenly illuminated and characters are just as suddenly brought to life. In both scenes, the action drops off as sharply as it began. The wine flows, the people dance and sing, the gaunt inhabitants of Saint Antoine appear as grotesques. Then the stage quickly returns to the quiet and emptiness that prevails before the wine-cask was broken. From the window of Tellson's Paris quarters, we look down with Jarvis Lorry as the courtyard is suddenly flooded with activity. The people are smeared with blood, as they were smeared with wine in the scene just mentioned; the grinding wheel spins hypnotically, and the reader's gaze is drawn down upon the sight and its dramatic force. Dickens' dramatic sense is remarkably evident in *A Tale,* and it is an artistic and potent stylistic device in his writing.

Question 9.

How does Dickens make use of irony in the novel?

Answer

Dickens is acutely aware of the presence of irony in life and the value of it in literature. In the character of Carton, several ironies have been embodied. Certainly, it is ironic that the finest moment of Carton's life comes on the occasion of his death. In death, his life has meaning; for that death redeems an otherwise wasted existence. It is ironic also that during the hours before the time he expects to be led to the guillotine, Charles Darnay never once turns his thoughts to Carton. Madame Defarge's death, as well, is touched with an ironic note. She is slain by her own weapon and also by the intense hate that had brought her to Lucie's lodgings in the first place. Barsad was a prosecution witness against Darnay in the Old Bailey and his testimony nearly convicted him. Here, in Paris, he becomes an essential instrument in Carton's plan for Darnay's escape. The skilful use of irony grants poignancy to any narrative, and Dickens incorporates it, particularly with Carton, in a way that focusses even greater attention upon that man's courageous act.

Bibliography

Baker, Ernest A. *The History of the English Novel,* Vol. 7. New York: Barnes & Noble, Inc., 1963.

Brown, Ivor. *Dickens in His Time.* London: Thomas Nelson and Sons, 1963.

Cary, John. *The Violent Effigy: A Study of Dickens' Imagination.* London: Faber & Faber, 1973.

Chesterton, Gilbert Keith. *Charles Dickens: A Critical Study.* New York: Dodd, Mead and Co., 1913.

Cockshut, A. O. J. *The Imagination of Charles Dickens.* New York: New York University Press, 1962.

Davis, Earle. *The Flint and the Flame.* Columbia, Missouri: University of Missouri Press, 1963.

Dyson, A. E. *Dickens* ("Modern Judgments Series"). London: Macmillan and Co., 1968.

Engel, Monroe. *The Maturity of Dickens.* Cambridge, Massachusetts: Harvard University Press, 1959.

Fenstermaker, John. *Charles Dickens, 1940-1975: An Index to Periodical Criticism.* Boston: G.K. Hall & Co., 1979.

Fielding, K. J. *Charles Dickens: A Critical Introduction.* New York: David McKay Co., 1958.

Ford, George H., and Lane, Lauriat, Jr., eds. *The Dickens Critics.* Ithaca: Cornell University Press, 1961.

Forster, John. *The Life of Charles Dickens,* 2 vols. London: J. M. Dent and Sons, Ltd. Also New York: E. P. Dutton and Co., Inc., 1927.

Gissing, George. *Critical Studies of the Works of Charles Dickens.* New York: Greenberg, Publishers, 1924.

House, Humphry. *The Dickens World,* 2nd ed. New York: Oxford University Press, 1960.

Jackson, T. A. *Charles Dickens: The Progress of a Radical.* New York: Haskell House Publishers Ltd., 1971.

Johnson, Edgar. *Charles Dickens: His Tragedy and Triumph,* 2 vols. Boston: Little, Brown and Co., 1965.

Manning, S. B. *Dickens as Satirist.* New Haven: Yale University Press, 1971.

Pearson, Hesketh. *Dickens: His Character, Comedy and Career.* New York: Harper and Brothers, 1949.

Pope-Hennessy, Una. *Charles Dickens.* London: Howell, Soskin, 1946.

Stirling, Nora. *Who Wrote the Classics?* New York: The John Day Co., 1965.

Wilson, Edmund. *The Wound and the Bow.* New York: Oxford University Press, 1929.

NOTES

NOTES

NOTES

NOTES